Sainsbury's Homebase Guide to

INDOOR GARDENING

Ken March

CONTENTS

NOTES
For convenience, ease-of-growing symbols have been incorporated in the A-Z sections. They can be interpreted as follows:
* Easy to grow houseplants
** Plants which require more than average care
*** Temperamental or difficult to grow plants

Published exclusively for
J Sainsbury plc
Stamford Street, London SE1 9LL
by Cathay Books
59 Grosvenor Street, London W1

First published 1983

ISBN 0 86178 195 3

Printed in Hong Kong

CHOOSING HOUSEPLANTS

Houseplants add colour and interest to any part of the home, whether chosen for the beauty of their foliage or the vividness of their flowers. But selecting a houseplant is not simply a matter of picking out the one that looks best in a shop display. By first giving a little thought to the plant, how it is displayed and where you want to keep it when you get it home, you will choose one that will adapt rapidly to its new environment.

WHERE TO BUY HOUSEPLANTS

The way in which plants for sale are displayed is a matter of great importance, and a point often overlooked. A great number of plants are bought on impulse, not surprising when you consider that it is the eye-catching quality of foliage and flowers that constitutes their appeal.

On occasions such as Mother's Day, Easter or Christmas, many of us solve a present problem with a colourful flowering houseplant. To catch the attention of passers-by, some retailers display their plants on the pavement. While this might be acceptable to many houseplants during the warm spring and summer months, and while hardier houseplants such as azaleas, primulas or jasmine might even tolerate such treatment during autumn and winter, it is not in the best interests of the plants. Many plants are so susceptible to fluctuations in temperature and particularly to chilling, they should never be displayed outside.

It is particularly unwise to buy any of the following from an outside display:

Anthurium	Gardenia
Aphelandra	Hibiscus
Begonia rex	Kentia
Beloperone	Maranta
Bromeliads	Neanthe
Columnea	Peperomia
Croton	Philodendron
Dieffenbachia	Poinsettia
Ferns	Saintpaulia
Fittonia	Stephanotis

The damage is not always obvious. You will often see poinsettias, for example, on a market stall at Christmas that appear to be in reasonable condition, and it is only when the plants are in their new home that the shock will show its effects. You then blame yourself for the problems that manifest themselves. Remember that many houseplants are raised at temperatures between 18-20°C (65-68°F), and sufficient harm can be done by transporting them to market in unheated lorries, without subjecting them further by exposure to cold draughts and icy winds. If tropical fish were treated like many houseplants of tropical origin, few would survive!

The best place to buy houseplants is likely to be a reputable shop or garden centre that displays the plants under conditions similar to those in which they were grown. The shop should be relatively warm and well lit whether by natural or artificial light. The best situation is a shop that has a heated glasshouse or an area well lit from roof-lights or large display windows. Ideally, the place where plants are sold should be one in which they can grow rather than just be stored. The staff should also know something about the plants and be able to offer you advice. Before you leave the shop, make sure your plants are individually wrapped to protect them against fluctuations in temperature.

HOW TO SELECT A HEALTHY PLANT

A weak, damaged plant is unlikely to survive long after you have bought it, so it is important to look for signs of neglect. Avoid plants which have leaves that are limp or browning at the edges, or appear to be falling from the plant. Drooping and spindly stems are other bad signs. If roots seem to be emerging from the drainage holes in the bottom of the pot, the plant is far too cramped and should have been repotted some time ago. Dry compost is a further indication of neglect. If you are buying a flowering plant, make sure you choose one with plenty of buds. If all of the flowers are already in bloom, you will not have a colourful display for long.

Look for plants with shiny, well-coloured leaves and strong, sturdy stems. Check that the compost is moist and make sure that the plant has no accompanying insects!

HOW TO POSITION HOUSEPLANTS

It is essential to choose a plant according to the position you intend it to occupy in the home. Finding a spare corner for something you have bought on impulse rarely leads to a success. The plants must be placed in the correct environment for successful growth. The appropriate environment means three conditions: the right amount of light, the right temperature and the proper level of humidity.

Study your home and decide where plants would really enhance the decor, then consider the environment. Is it a dark corner or a light windowsill, for example? Is the atmosphere moist or dry, and how does the temperature vary? You may even be at the stage where you can plan an interior decorating scheme to take into account the special needs of plants you want to grow! By reading the label or examining the plant for a few key points, you can identify the right conditions for the plant and its place in your home before you buy it.

The things to look for are related to three factors that constitute a correct environment: temperature, light, and humidity. Finally, remember that the first week or so in a new home is critical for a plant, so take particular care while it is adapting to its new environment.

TEMPERATURE

Observation alone cannot tell you what temperature a plant prefers; this information should be given on its label. If you buy from a shop where the plants do not have care labels, an assistant should be able to tell you or look it up. Don't be afraid to ask. Although plants have different optimum temperatures, it is impossible to cater for each plant's individual requirements in the ordinary home. This situation is exaggerated in winter when we attempt to heat our homes to a reasonable level of comfort, and in summer when we are at the mercy of unpredictable weather.

What makes temperature so important? The correct temperature enables the plants to grow at the correct rate, building up strength as they mature. Too low a temperature, and growth slows down; too warm, and plants can become spindly. But we are not dealing here with delicate greenhouse specimens; the plants described in the following pages are adaptable to some degree, and an average temperature of about 18-20°C (65-68°F) will suit most of them. Obviously, during the summer months, it is likely to get warmer than this, but most plants will adapt.

It is often a fluctuating temperature that causes the most problems and this can be more critical than a lower steady temperature. Widely fluctuating temperatures are most likely to occur in winter when rooms are heated during the day then left to cool at night. A sudden change in temperature can also occur on a windowsill or near a door either by draught or drop in exterior temperature at night. A plant on a windowsill will be cut off from the room's warmth when you draw the curtains at nightfall. This dramatic change from warmth to cold can severely affect some plants, causing them to shed their leaves prematurely. Croton, *Ficus benjamina*, poinsettia and hibiscus are particularly vulnerable. Aim for a steady temperature; surprisingly, many plants that would react badly to fluctuations between hot and cold will adapt well to a stable lower temperature of around 15°C (60°F).

Remember that humidity level is affected by temperature. The warmer it gets, the drier the atmosphere is; the cooler, the more moist.

The temperatures recommended in this book are ideal. Many plants will tolerate lower temperatures if the compost is kept slightly drier than normal.

LIGHT

All plants require light to grow, apart from primitive plants like fungi that manage without it. Light is a source of energy that is absorbed by the green pigment, chlorophyll, in the leaves and used to manufacture foods for the plant with the aid of water, a solution of mineral nutrients, and oxygen. This is the process known as photosynthesis.

Plants chosen to suit their environment.
ABOVE: Cacti on a dry, sunny windowsill.
LEFT: Hydrangeas in a well-lit, humid bathroom.

The amount of light needed by plants varies according to the species, and also affects their appearance and condition. Many plants with very dark green leaves are generally happier with a lower intensity of light, away from windows and more in the centre of the room. Because they have more chlorophyll in their leaves they are better able to absorb the smaller amount of light available. It is not surprising, therefore, that when some dark green leaved plants are placed next to a window, they often turn a paler green. It seems that the plant reduces its light-collecting capability because there is more light available.

Some plants that are used to a lower light level react adversely to direct sunlight. They may turn an unhealthy yellow colour, or suffer from sun scorch, when patches on the foliage dehydrate and turn brown.

Flowering plants need a well-lit position to flower successfully.

Plants that are happier with lower light intensities are:

Anthurium	Hedera (green varieties)
Aspidistra	Howea
Bromeliads	Hoya
Cissus	Maranta
Columnea	Monstera
Dracaena marginata	Neanthe
Ferns	Philodendron
Ficus	Phoenix
Fittonia	Rhoicissus
Gardenia	Saintpaulia

Plants with variegated or highly coloured leaves are generally happier with a higher level of light and prefer to be close to a light source. The colours of these plants are at their best in spring and summer when light levels are at their highest; it is then that the plants reduce the green pigment in favour of brighter hues. During autumn and winter the colour fades again to green; with less light available, the plant needs to produce more light-collecting chlorophyll to maintain healthy growth.

If you place a plant with variegated or highly coloured leaves away from light or in the centre of a room, you may be disappointed with the poor coloration. To bring back the bright colours, put the plant near a window.

Many flowering plants like high light intensities irrespective of leaf colour; they probably need the light to reflect the colours of the flowers in order to attract pollinating insects.

Plants that like higher light intensities are:

Ananas	Dieffenbachia
Aphelandra	*Dracaena deremensis*
Azalea	*Dracaena terminalis*
Begonia rex	Hedera (variegated varieties)
Beloperone	Hibiscus
Cacti and other succulents	Hydrangea
Chlorophytum	Impatiens
Chrysanthemum	Jasmine
Croton	Poinsettia
Cyclamen	Polyanthus

Artificial lighting of houseplants is a fascinating extension of indoor gardening, and rewards closer examination. A bottle garden is an excellent subject to be lit by fluorescent lighting, extending the range of light-loving plants into dark corners.

HUMIDITY

While many plants prefer to live in a moisture-laden atmosphere, others seem to thrive without it. Whatever the case, most houses are far less humid than the plant's natural atmosphere. This is a point you will appreciate if you visit a botanic garden, or a good nursery or garden centre and walk into the glasshouse where the houseplants are displayed. The air is warm and damp, sometimes uncomfortably so – a situation which many plants prefer.

Luckily, it is not as difficult as it seems to provide the correct conditions, and does not involve converting your home into a sauna! All you need to know is which conditions suit your plants. As a general rule, plants that have fairly thin leaves prefer a more humid environment and are more susceptible to an atmosphere that is warm and dry. This is because thin leaves cannot hold much water and dry out quite rapidly. In a warm, dry atmosphere they will suffer: the leaves curl up, and the extremities of the plant that are most susceptible – the leaf tips and edges – dehydrate.

Plants particularly sensitive to a warm, dry situation are:

Aspidistra	Fittonia
Azalea	Gardenia
Begonia	Hedera
Beloperone	Hibiscus
Chlorophytum	Hydrangea
Chrysanthemum	Howea
Cissus	Impatiens
Columnea	Jasmine
Dieffenbachia	Maranta
Dracaena	Neanthe
Ferns	Polyanthus
Ficus benjamina	Rhoicissus
Ficus pumila	Tradescantia

Even some plants that have fleshier leaves, such as saintpaulia, also prefer a more humid environment. Conversely, many of the tougher, leathery leaved or succulent types of plant tolerate, and in some cases prefer, a drier environment. Those that tolerate it do so because their thick leaves have a greater water storage capacity. Those that prefer a drier situation, do so because these are the conditions prevailing in their native habitat and their leaves have adapted by losing less moisture through their pores.

Moisture-loving plants being grouped together in a bowl of moist peat to help maintain a humid environment – Dieffenbachia, two Begonia Rex varieties, and Maranta leuconeura 'Tricolor' (rear).

Examples of plants that can tolerate a drier atmosphere are:

Ananas	Croton
Araucaria	*Ficus elastica*
Bromeliads	Monstera
Cacti and succulents	*Peperomia magnoliaefolia*

Having identified some plants with particular likes and dislikes, the next step is catering for their needs. Providing a dry atmosphere is not usually difficult, particularly in centrally heated homes. The problem comes with trying to humidify the atmosphere. One way is to purchase a humidifier, Another less costly method is to spray plants that are particularly sensitive to dry air with a fine mist of tepid water once or twice a day, no more. This method is acceptable if you can remember to do it regularly. There are two other practical solutions that are less trouble.

Place the plant, in its pot, in a tray or bowl of moist peat or sphagnum moss which is more or the less the same diameter as the plant's spread. If you keep the peat or moss damp, the moisture evaporating from it will help to prevent the leaves of the plant from drying out. Another method is simply to group together plants that like relatively high humidity: this alone helps to reduce water loss from the leaves. The best solution is a combination of the two if you have the space: group several plants together in a large tray or bowl of moist peat or sphagnum moss.

PLANT CARE

Each plant could be said to have its own 'personality'; this is demonstrated when two similar plants are grown side by side. Even with identical treatment, you will find that one dries out before the other or grows at a different rate. This goes to show that while a general guide is useful, it must be interpreted to suit an individual plant's needs. The longer you keep your plants, the better you will get to know them, so don't be surprised if one day you find yourself talking to them!

A healthy plant needs more than a congenial environment or 'atmosphere' in which to thrive. Also crucial to its continuing welfare are the maintenance tasks of watering, feeding, cleaning, pruning, re-potting and pest and disease control. Propagation is a skill worth mastering as many plants reproduce easily and will provide you with new young plants to increase your display. Daily you will learn more and your confidence as an indoor gardener will grow – along with the plants.

WATERING

The majority of houseplants that die do so because they have been overwatered. What often happens is that a plant – let's say a rubber plant – is kept moist according to the label's instructions. All goes well for a few weeks and then you notice that the plant has started to wilt. Naturally you think it must be dry and water it. A few days later, you notice that it is still wilting and water it yet again. The plant continues to deteriorate, although inspection proves that the compost is still moist. Finally the leaves start to drop off until all that remains is a long, bare stem with two or three leaves at the top. What has happened? Ironically, the plant is suffering (and may expire) from lack of water because it has been overwatered. The more water that is poured into the compost, the more air is squeezed out – and air in the compost is essential. Too much water at the expense of air suffocates the roots; in this condition they stagnate, cannot absorb water, and the plant starts to dehydrate. To prevent this happening, and as a general rule only, allow the compost to become almost dry between waterings. This rule does not apply to plants that should be kept moist all the time, such as azalea, most ferns and hydrangea.

To check for dryness, don't just look at the surface of the compost; while the compost in a plastic pot tends to dry out at the surface it may still be quite moist below. If the compost is dry at a depth of 2-3 cm (1 inch), water is required. Press the compost lightly with a finger – you will soon learn by sense of touch whether the plant needs watering.

If the compost feels moist, don't water for the time being, unless of course the plant is one of the rare exceptions that likes wet roots.

Most plants can be watered over the surface of the compost. Use tepid water or water at room temperature because cold water can give the roots a shock. Let the water drain into a saucer and leave it for about 20 minutes. Pour away the surplus water and leave the plant standing in a dry saucer. Do not leave the plant sitting in a saucer of water indefinitely.

Certain plants must be watered from below. Amongst them are fleshy-leaved plants such as saintpaulia, *Begonia rex* and cyclamen which have a tendency to rot if water sits on the foliage or round the neck of the plant. Pour water into a saucer and after about 20 minutes, pour away the surplus.

Azaleas and hydrangeas prefer to be watered by being lowered into a bucket of tepid water until most of the air has bubbled up. When the bubbling stops, remove the pot and leave it to drain.

Many people are convinced that only rainwater must be used, but most houseplants are content with tap water. There are some exceptions that prefer 'softer' water, ie. water relatively free of lime. Amongst them are azaleas, gardenias and hydrangeas. Boiled, cooled tap water is just about acceptable as a substitute, but for best results you will need to indulge these plants with clean rainwater.

Finally, remember that most plants require less water in winter, when they are 'resting', than in summer when they are actively growing. Exceptions are the few plants which rest in summer and grow in winter.

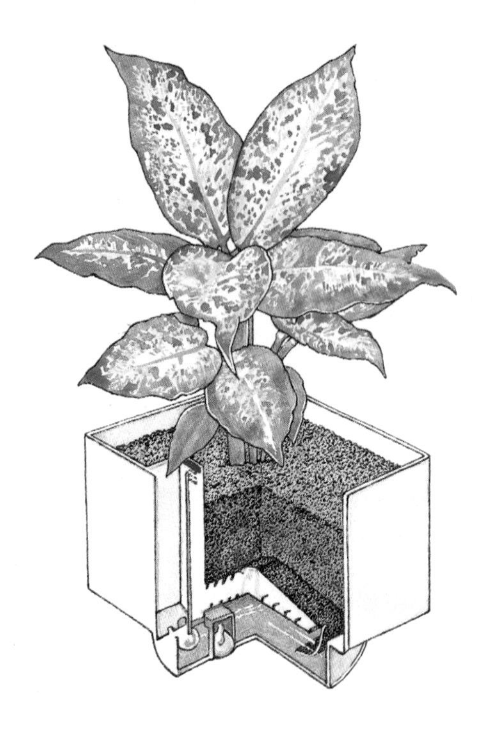

LEFT: Self-watering container – particularly useful during holidays. Water is drawn up from the reservoir by the wick, which distributes moisture through the soil by capillary action.

RIGHT: Removing dust from Ficus elastica leaves by wiping them gently with a damp cotton wool pad. More delicate Saintpaulia leaves are cleaned by spraying with tepid water.

FEEDING

Plants can get by on water alone for some time, for there is usually a reasonable supply of plant food in the compost to sustain them for a while. However this food supply will need supplementing in due course. A peat-based compost will begin to run out of nutrients relatively quickly – as soon as a month after potting.

The time of the year should affect your feeding programme. Plants are generally less active in the winter and therefore need less food. Overfeeding with most houseplant fertilizers can lead to a harmful build-up of nutrient salts in the compost. Fertilizers which depend partly on temperature for their action, do not cause such a problem.

The correct time to feed most plants is during spring and summer, when they are active and need nutrients to encourage healthy growth. How often to feed depends upon the situation of the plant and the type of fertilizer, but generally once every two weeks should be sufficient for liquid feeds. Other fertilizers can be applied less frequently. Most liquid fertilizers are sold in the form of liquid concentrates, but there are also soluble powders. These should be diluted according to manufacturer's directions before application; only a few can be applied 'neat' to the compost and then watered in. Liquid fertilizers should be applied in place of a routine watering, unless the plant is dry at the roots. In this case, moisten the compost first with ordinary water. If undiluted fertilizer reaches very thirsty roots it can cause irreparable damage.

There are a number of other neat ways of feeding plants that could save you time. Slow-release fertilizers in the form of little tablets or sticks are inserted into the compost. These gradually dissolve and feed the plants over a period of weeks or months. A recent introduction are 'controlled release' granules. These only release their fertilizers when it is warm enough for the plant to utilize them. The release of nutrients continues over a period of around six months, the exact length of time depending on the temperature.

The type of fertilizer that you use will depend very much on whether the plants you are growing are foliage or flowering houseplants. Foliage houseplants can be fed with any of the range of proprietary houseplant fertilizers that are rich in nitrogen. Flowering plants need a feed rich in potassium, such as a tomato fertilizer. This also helps to produce a stocky plant rather than one that is soft and 'leafy'. Always use tomato fertilizer at about half-strength for houseplants. Do not be tempted into using a stronger mix in the belief that you will get more flowers – you will probably damage the plant.

Whichever type of fertilizer you select, never overfeed a plant. The application of more fertilizer than is recommended will not make the plant grow better or faster. Too much fertilizer can damage or kill the plant.

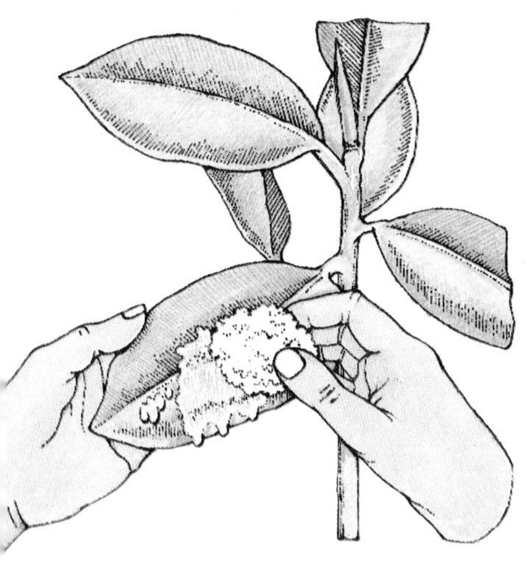

CLEANING

Because houseplants tend to gather dust they can look rather dull and neglected. Dust on the leaves is not healthy; the dust particles can block the plants' breathing pores (called stomata) and reduce their vigour. It is therefore important to clean plants occasionally to remove dust and dirt. You should only clean the plant for its own benefit, not your own: many people believe that an attractive and healthy plant is one with highly glossed leaves, but this is nonsense. A healthy plant has clean, bright leaves with a natural sheen, not one applied out of a bottle.

While there are some useful plant cleaning aids on the market that remove dust, either on a moistened cloth or a pad of damp cotton wool, there are some oily shining materials available that simply mask the grime and suffocate the leaves. Aerosols are of no benefit either – they too simply mask the dust. To remove dust either simply spray houseplants with tepid water or, for the tougher-leaved specimens, gently wipe the leaves with a cotton wool pad or soft cloth moistened with tepid water or even a little milk and water. One of the proprietary leaf-shine materials can be used on tougher-leaved plants such as ficus, monstera, hedera, dracaena and philodendron, but never apply these materials to soft- or thin-leaved plants such as ferns. Do not use oils such as olive oil or cooking oil; these will block the plant's pores.

Some plants are very difficult to clean, particularly those with hairy leaves, such as saintpaulia; those with crinkly, fleshy leaves such as *Begonia rex;* or those with a sensitive coating to the leaves or fronds, such as aechmea or platycerium. None of these should be wiped; instead give the leaves a very fine mist of tepid water.

PRUNING

Do not be too concerned about pruning and trimming your plants. Unlike many garden plants, houseplants do not need regular pruning. It will only be necessary occasionally to keep them tidily in check, or perhaps to provide cuttings from which to propagate.

Flowering houseplants should be deadheaded regularly. Do this by hand: nip the spent flowers between your forefinger and thumb: they should come away easily; if not, leave them on the plant for a day or two before trying again.

The best time to trim plants is in spring and summer when they are in active growth. This way they quickly re-grow and fill in the gaps. It is important to make a clean cut to minimize the risk of disease setting in or of pests attacking. For this reason the tool you use is important. Most houseplants can be trimmed with sharp scissors or a sharp knife; tougher-stemmed plants call for a pair of secateurs. Plants with very soft, fleshy, succulent and delicate stems such as saintpaulia are best

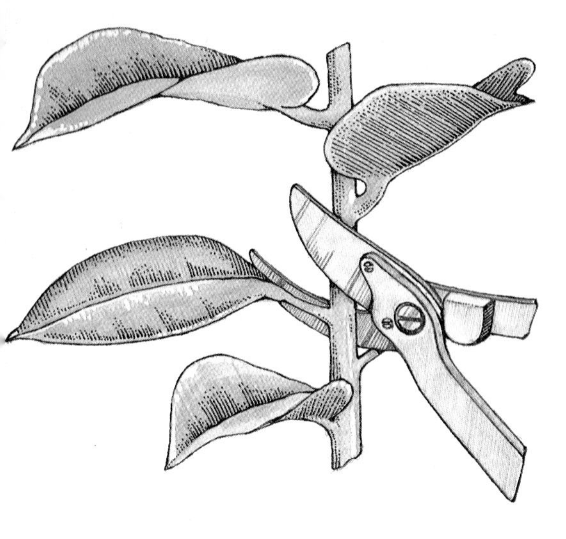

Pruning Ficus elastica (rubber plant) to maintain a well-shaped plant, and to provide cuttings for propagation. A slanting cut is made through this thick stem about 2.5 cm (1 inch) above a leaf, with a pair of 'parrot beak' secateurs.

trimmed with a sharp knife. Scissors or secateurs might cause bruising. Plants with woodier or fibrous stems that are fairly thin, such as *Ficus pumila* or hedera, are best trimmed with sharp scissors. Some plants have fairly thick or woody stems, such as ficus elastica, monstera, and dracaena. For these you will need to use a pair of secateurs of the 'parrot beak' type.

In most cases, the operation of trimming or pruning is very simple, involving a cut about 1 cm (½ inch) above a leaf. If you leave a longer stump, dieback could occur; if you leave it much shorter you could damage the leaf.

Some plants require a little extra care. Ficus and poinsettia ooze a sticky sap that trickles down the stem after cutting, but this can be controlled by lightly sprinkling ground charcoal or very fine sand on the wound.

If you prune a specimen such as a dracaena, ficus, monstera or croton with a stem more than 2.5 cm (1 inch) in diameter, use a pruning sealing compound to help the wound to heal quickly and avoid any possible infection that could gain entry through the cut.

REPOTTING

Some plants need annual repotting because they increase in size quickly; eventually all plants need to be repotted, whether for the benefit of providing fresh compost and nutrients or to ease a problem of instability. To carry this out successfully, you will need to choose the right compost, a pot of the correct size, and the most appropriate time.

A plant that has just been purchased is normally perfectly happy in its pot for at least a year; repotting sooner should not be necessary and could shock the plant. Sickly plants should not be repotted either, even though you may think that fresh compost will help its recovery. The shock of repotting may finish off an ailing specimen.

Repotting should only be carried out on healthy plants that have outgrown their pots or are running out of nutrients. The best time to do this is mid-spring to mid-summer when the plant is in active growth and can cope with the sudden change. Winter repotting may prove fatal to a dormant plant, which will react badly to any disturbance.

Do not over-pot. If you give a plant too much compost you will be giving it more water than it needs. Select a pot that is one or two sizes larger than the old one. As a guide, go from a 9 cm (3½ inch) pot into a 13 cm (5 inch) one; from a 13 cm (5 inch) to an 18 cm (7 inch); from an 18 cm (7 inch) to a 25 cm (10 inch) pot, and so on.

The type of pot is up to you. Plastic pots are cleaner, lighter and easier to handle, but tend to hold water longer and because they are non-porous do not allow the compost to 'breathe'. Because clay pots are heavier they are more stable, but they are more easily broken and tend to get dirty. The best thing about them is that because they are made of a natural, porous substance the compost stays in better condition.

The right compost is very important: you will achieve far better results by using a proprietary compost than by attempting to mix your own. If you do decide to mix your own, never use unsterilized garden soil; it might be all right for garden plants, but is usually too full of diseases and weed seed to use for potting a houseplant. A good proprietary compost will provide the plant with a supply of nutrients for

A simple method of repotting, using a pot the same size as the outgrown one as a guide. This enables the new pot to be filled to the correct height with compost, leaving a hollow just the right size for the plant's root ball.

at least 3 months. It will also ensure adequate aeration of the roots, and drainage.

There are two main types of compost: loam-based (containing soil) and peat-based (soil-less). The peat-based type usually contains a mixture of sand or vermiculite in with the peat. Choose a reputable brand, preferably with a high peat content to encourage good fibrous root growth. Do not be tempted by mixes that look good value for money if you do not recognize the name or formulation. It takes experience to mix a good, well-balanced product.

If you have a large plant that needs help to sit firmly in its pot, use a loam-based compost to provide weight and balance. All-peat composts are light in weight when dry and will exacerbate the problem.

There are several ways to repot a plant, but the following method is a favourite: it works well and is fun. Assemble all the materials you need: the plant in its existing pot; new pot; compost; a can of water. For prickly cacti, you will need a pair of thick leather gloves for protection. Water the plant then place it to one side.

Take the new pot and place some compost in the bottom. Use the old pot with the plant still in it (or one the same size) to check the height by placing it inside the new one. If it is too high, take some compost out, if too low put in more compost. When the two are level at the top, hold the old pot in the centre of the new one and fill in the gap between them with compost, using the old pot as a mould. When the new pot is full of compost, press down the old pot squarely to firm it, then remove the pot with a gentle twist. You should be left with a neat hole the size and shape of the old pot.

Remove the plant gently from the old pot with all the compost clinging to the roots; you may need to tap the rim of the pot against a firm surface to loosen the plant. Place the root-ball in the new pot, then tap on the floor or a table to settle the compost, topping up if required. Water the fresh compost immediately and place the plant in a warm, partly shaded position.

For the first few weeks, take care not to overwater the plant, for there will be a larger volume of compost and therefore more water for the plant to absorb. It will not be necessary to feed for at least a month.

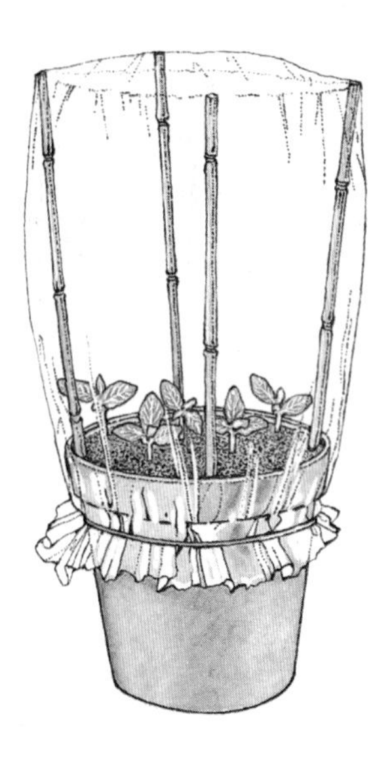

ABOVE: A polythene bag is used to assist the growth of these Fittonia argyroneura (little snakeskin plant) cuttings. The bag is supported by stakes and sealed under the rim of the pot to create a micro-environment.

PROPAGATION

The propagation of individual plants is dealt with in the appropriate entry in the A-Z section. There are, however, some general guidelines and the main methods are shown here.

Compost is important. Use a seed or cutting compost, as these have a low concentration of nutrients to avoid harming the roots, and an open texture to encourage the formation of fibrous roots.

Rooting hormones stimulate root production. Some contain a fungicide to reduce the likelihood of rots destroying the cutting before it roots properly. Rooting hormones are available in powder or liquid form. Liquids adhere better, but powders can be made to do so just as well by dipping the end of the cutting in water before dipping it into the powder. Insert the cutting gently into the compost and do not make the compost too compact around the stem.

To create a micro-environment in which the cuttings will have enough warmth, humidity, and protection from draughts while they are developing roots, cover them in their pot (or tray) with a polythene bag large enough to leave an adequate air space around them.

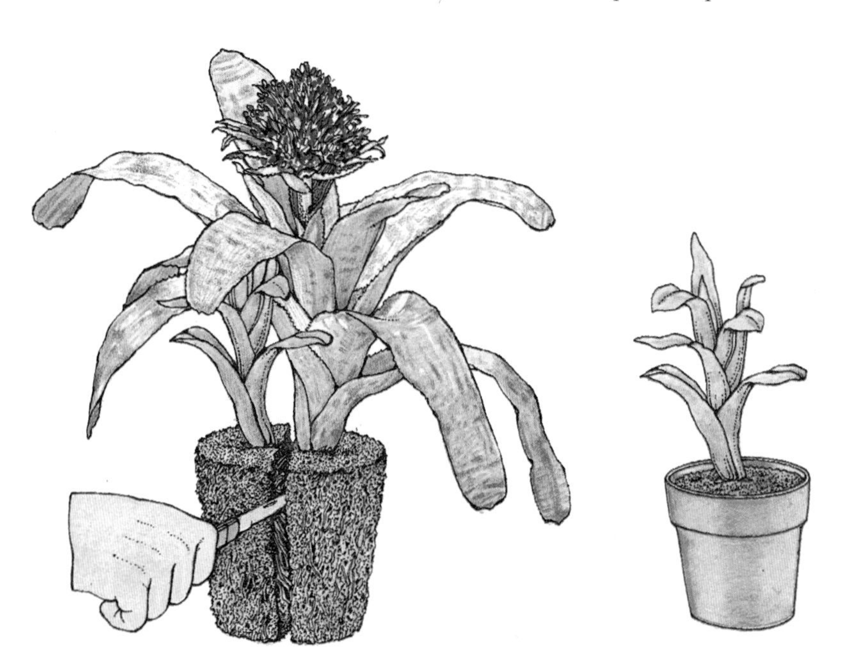

LEFT: Propagation by offsets. The offset produced by this Aechmea fasciata is carefully prised away when it is about a third of the height of its parent and potted up singly.

ABOVE (TOP): Propagation by stem cuttings. A 10 cm (4 inch) cutting is taken from the Ficus elastica with a leaf attached, and potted in a mixture of sand and peat. The leaf is secured to a stake by an elastic band for support.

ABOVE (MIDDLE): Propagation by leaf cuttings. A mature healthy leaf is cut from the saintpaulia, with the leaf stalk attached and inserted in a pot of seed compost. The base of the leaf must be clear of the compost.

ABOVE (LOWER): Propagation by tip cuttings. A stem cutting with several leaves attached is taken from the top of a mature Poinsettia, and potted up in a peat and sand mixture.

PESTS & DISEASES

If a plant appears to be unhealthy, it is most likely suffering from a physiological disorder. It may be receiving too much or too little water or light, or you may be keeping it at the wrong temperature.

However, occasionally houseplants may be attacked by pests or diseases; weak plants are particularly vulnerable. If you detect either pests or diseases on a plant take prompt action to control the problem. The following descriptions will help you identify the infestation, and cope with it.

Before using any pesticides, read the manufacturer's instructions carefully and take their advice on how to use the product and what safeguards should be observed. Pesticides can be poisonous to small children, pets and wildlife. Store them in a safe place and never transfer them to other containers. Rinse out cans or sprays thoroughly after use. Certain chemicals may also damage some varieties of plants, so observe recommendations.

APHIDS

Aphids are more commonly known as greenfly, but there are many different varieties including blackfly, and others of different colours and with different tastes. They have sharp, spear-like feeding tubes which they stab into soft plant tissue to consume sap. The damage caused by aphids is usually severe and infestation tends to increase dramatically. Because aphids feed on developing growth and new shoots, the adverse effects can be seen long after the pests themselves have been eliminated. The feeding tubes of the insect penetrate well into the leaves forming inside the new shoot.

Control: Deal with aphids as soon as you spot them before they cause any major damage. They reproduce with amazing speed. When infestations are at a low level they can be dealt with relatively easily by being rinsed off under a gentle flow of tepid water. Alternatively, aphids can be eliminated by spraying with

Aphids on Impatiens

Botrytis on Begonia rex

pirimicarb, permethrin, malathion or pyrethrum at weekly intervals for about three weeks.

BOTRYTIS

Botrytis, or grey mould fungus, can be a real nuisance to plants such as cyclamen, saintpaulia and other fleshy leaved plants. Generally, botrytis starts as a fungal attack growing on dead or damaged leaves or flowers, covering the tissue with a fluffy grey mould. As the level of infection increases, it may attack healthy tissue. Indeed sometimes it will attack healthy tissue to begin with. Once the infection has reached this stage, it can kill a plant within a few days or so. The fungus spreads its infection by releasing clouds of greyish coloured spores when the foliage is disturbed or fanned by air currents.

Control: Control is best achieved by a combination of cultural and chemical treatment. First of all, any dead or dying leaves or flowers should be removed. Second, the application of a fungicide such as benomyl or sulphur may help to prevent an infection from occurring if applied once every two months or so. However, if an infection is recognized, a weekly or two-weekly application of a suitable fungicide involving about two or three applications may eradicate the problem if you manage to catch it in the early stages.

MEALY BUGS

Mealy bugs show themselves as white, woolly patches on the underside of leaves or in the gap between the leaf stalk and the main stem. In these patches the young mealy bugs are incubated. Adult mealy bugs look like small white woodlice and move rather slowly. Infestations of mealy bugs are usually localized and spread slowly. Often only one plant is affected. Mealy bugs can cause severe damage, particularly to developing growth.

Control: Where the level of attack is low, use spot-treatment. Dip a cotton wool bud into methylated spirits and dab each patch of 'wool' and each adult. Treat the entire plant and repeat the treatment after about one or two weeks. If the infestation is of a high level and affects several plants, you may need to spray the plants with an insecticide. Use malathion or permethrin two or three times at two-weekly intervals.

Mealy bugs on Chrysanthemum

Mildew on Rhoicissus rhomboidea

MILDEW

Mildew is a fungal disease which often affects garden roses. Powdery or downy mildews cover infected leaves with white dusty or fluffy patches. Fortunately, mildew does not affect many indoor plants, but once the infection has established itself it is difficult to eradicate.

Control: The best method of control is prevention, applying a fungicide such as sulphur once every two to four weeks. If infection occurs and no preventive measure has been taken, apply a fungicide such as benomyl or sulphur once or twice a week for about a month or so.

RED SPIDER MITES

The tiny red spider mites can cause serious damage to houseplants. They live on the undersides of leaves where they munch away at the tissue causing severe discoloration, leaf cupping and inhibition of growth. Sometimes the mites spin crude webs from one part of the plant to another, or from plant to plant. These webs act as bridges, allowing the pests to move across to new pastures.

The mites are normally straw-coloured, turning red when temperatures drop and they go into hibernation. Red spider mites thrive under warm, dry conditions and dislike excessively moist conditions or low temperatures.

Control: Spray tepid water under and over the leaves during warm, dry conditions. Chemical controls can be effective if regularly administered at weekly or two-weekly intervals for about a month. Use malathion, permethrin or dimethoate.

ROOT MEALY BUGS

Unfortunately, by the time you realize that a plant is affected by root mealy bugs, the infestation is probably quite high and difficult to control. Root mealy bugs live on the roots of plants in the compost around the outer edge of the plant's root ball and are therefore difficult to detect. Infestation inhibits the affected plant growth, starving and stunting the plants and often causing yellowing of the leaves. White woolly patches like those of mealy bugs are found around the roots.

Control: Root mealy bugs can only be effectively dealt with by dipping the plant's root ball (still in its pot) into a solution of malathion.

Red spider mites on Tradescantia

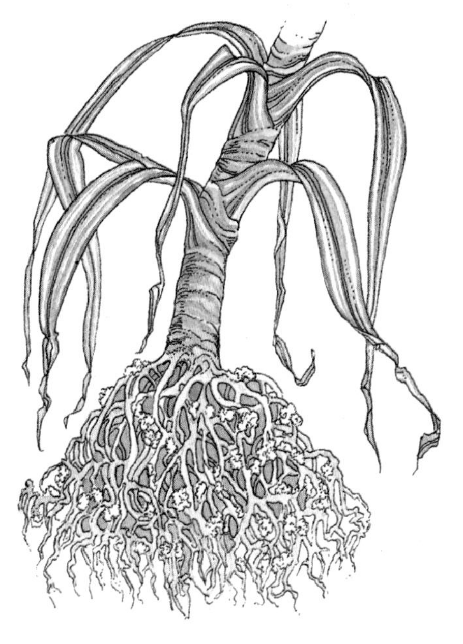

Root mealy bugs on Dracaena

Repeat this treatment two or three times at two-week intervals.

SCALE INSECTS

Scale insects look like blisters or swellings on the leaves or plant stems, blending in well and often defying early recognition. When young, scale insects are straw-coloured and oval in shape. As they mature, they become rounder. Eventually the outer cover hardens and turns dark brown. The eggs are incubated inside this 'scale' before the young insects hatch out and go their own way. Scale insects usually prefer to feed on the undersides of leaves and fleshy stems. Once they have found a suitable situation they rarely move again. As their numbers increase, severe damage to plant tissue causes deformed growth. Since scale insects do not move far infections are often isolated to single plants. However, where several plants are grown in an arrangement, they may spread.

Control: The control of scale insects is not easy. While the young and feeding adults may be killed by the application of a chemical such as malathion or dimethoate, the eggs remain protected in the hardened cases. For this reason, it is a good idea to scrape off the visible 'scales'. Two or three applications of insecticide at two-weekly intervals coupled with removal of visible scales should eradicate this pest.

WHITEFLY

Whiteflies look like small moths. They live on the underside of leaves and there lay eggs which, when hatched, look like scales on the leaves. They have a fairly static life feeding off the sap from the plants. Their sticky excretion encourages a mould that looks like fine white dust. The adults fly off as soon as a leaf is disturbed, settling back on the plant a few seconds later. Although only a few whiteflies will cause little damage, they increase fast, and when the population is high, they mottle the leaves and reduce the plant's overall vigour. Warm dry conditions encourage breeding, but whitefly can survive cooler conditions.

Control: To eliminate whitefly you will have to be persistent. Spray once or twice a week for four to six weeks to kill the adults as soon as they hatch from the scales and before they can lay more eggs. Permethrin, pyrethrum or malathion can provide an effective solution.

Scale insects on Stephanotis

White fly on Saintpaulia

PLANT DISPLAY

While many houseplants are grown very effectively in isolation, the scope for adding a little more excitement to their display is almost endless. One of the simplest ways of enhancing the appearance of a houseplant lies in the choice of container.

CONTAINERS

The most common plant container in use today is the plastic pot. It is light, clean, easy to handle, fairly resilient, but has the effect of holding in moisture longer. The old-fashioned clay pot is beginning to make a comeback, having fallen out of favour because it is heavier, tends to get dirty and grow algae on the outside, is rather more difficult to handle and more easily broken if dropped. For all its disadvantages, however, the clay pot is a super container for plants. Many people will contend that the plastic pot is as good as the clay, but only the clay pot has the useful attribute of allowing air and moisture to pass through its porous sides. Its greater weight can be turned to advantage, as it will keep tall and top-heavy plants more safely anchored.

Whichever type of pots you choose, ensure that they are free-draining, where possible, and are placed on plastic saucers. Containers without drainage holes can be used but they are more difficult to manage because they make it easy to overwater.

If you decide to plant your houseplants in decorative troughs or boxes, take a few precautions to safeguard your home as well as your plants! Not all containers are waterproof and some that are made from a very coarse style of pottery occasionally leak. Wooden ones will certainly not hold water. It may be necessary to protect your furnishings and carpets.

Unglazed pottery containers that might leak may either be painted inside with a glass-fibre resin solution, or lined with one or two layers of thick-gauge polythene. Trim off the polythene just below the rim of the container but above the surface of the compost that you will eventually place in it.

Wooden containers will need a coat of clear polyurethane varnish on the inside before lining with thick polythene in the way already described.

Before filling any such container with compost, place some pieces of charcoal in the bottom to a depth of about 2.5 cm (1 inch). This aids drainage and prevents stagnation.

PLANT ARRANGEMENTS

There is no end to what you can do to get the best from your plants – with a little imagination. You need not be limited to the obvious possibilities of plants in individual containers. Mixed arrangements are a good idea provided that you choose plants that like similar conditions. Unfortunately, many of the bowl gardens that are on sale at Easter and Christmas are planted with a mixture of varieties that, while they look good together, do not have the same cultural requirements. Inevitably, one or two thrive at the expense of the rest and you have to split up the arrangement to save the plants. Careful plant selection will avoid this.

It is not even necessary to make a permanent planting. You can fill a large container with peat or sphagnum moss and simply place an arrangement of plants, still in their pots, in the mixture. It can be quickly assembled, changed at will and embellished with pieces of driftwood, moss, stones or cork bark. In this type of arrangement, water the plants individually and do not be misled by the peat looking dry or moist in the container. As the plants are still in their pots they need to be treated separately and do not take any significant amount of moisture from the peat.

You will often find that plants grouped together grow better. This is because they conserve moisture around themselves, producing their own microclimate. Bottle gardens embody this principle perfectly. In this case the level of humidity is maintained inside a container such as a carboy, goldfish bowl, aquarium or even an old sweet or pickle jar. The choice of plants is important. They should be varieties that will thrive in a humid environment, are slow-growers, and preferably non-flowering (essential for a 'sealed' garden). Flowers that drop on to the compost may rot.

Useful plants for bottle gardens are cryptanthus, small ferns, maranta, fittonia and *Ficus pumila*.

To make a bottle garden, place about 2.5 cm (1 inch) of charcoal in the bottom of the container before adding the appropriate amount of potting compost. Decide on the positioning of the plants in advance, as it may be awkward to change them afterwards. Where access is restricted, as in a carboy, make special planting tools for the delicate job of planting up. Use a dessert spoon tied to a long stick as an improvised long-handled trowel, a table fork tied to a long stick as a plant-positioning tool, and a cotton reel wedged on to a long stick as a tamper to firm the compost down gently around each plant. Whatever container you choose, water the plants and the compost with a fine spray after planting up, but do not overwater.

ABOVE: Training Ficus pumila up cane supports, using rings to secure the stems to their stakes. For maximum effect leave some stems trailing.
OPPOSITE: A fine example of a bottle garden in a carboy.

Containers that can be stoppered, or closed in some way, should be left open for a few weeks to settle down. Even after stoppering or putting on the cover, you may need to leave the top off for short periods at first to remove excess condensation. This will not be necessary once 'balance' has been achieved, although it's a good idea to open the container occasionally to change the atmosphere and prevent stagnation. A properly sealed bottle garden will not need watering as the condensation 'recycles' the water. An 'unstoppered' container will need regular attention and is best regarded as a means of displaying plants together, rather than a controlled environment.

While floor-space can be taken up with tubs, troughs, pots and bottle gardens, the ceiling space should not be forgotten. There are a number of plants that are particularly effective in hanging pots. The obvious choices are tradescantia and chlorophytum, but *Ficus pumila*, *Hoya bella*, platycerium, hedera, nephrolepis or columnea are also worth trying. Each will make a startling display in its own right. Hanging containers must be leakproof, and should be so designed and positioned that it is easy to get at them to apply water and check that compost and plant are in good condition.

TRAINING PLANTS

Many plants are capable of growing without special support, but others need help to look their best. Plants that require support because of their great size can often manage with a sturdy bamboo cane or plant stake inserted deep into the compost and then secured to the stem with plant ties. Canes and stakes may, however, need replacing eventually; if you want a permanent support for a very large specimen you could use a piece of plastic pipe. Plastic pipes sold for plumbing purposes by builders' merchants are often unobtrusively brown or grey and make good plant supports. Trellis can also be used indoors to good effect for training and supporting climbing plants. A suitable alternative for less vigorous species

might be a framework of small bamboo canes or plant stakes. A pliant cane hoop is another possibility.

When you attach a plant to its support, do not use thin wire or string as this may cut through the stems. There are several proprietary tying-in systems available, from paper-covered metal twists for fine-stemmed plants, gardening twine for sturdier specimens, and hessian strips for giant-sized plants.

Whatever support system you decide on, think carefully before making any permanent fixtures for your indoor garden: is spraying them likely to stain wall or furniture, or will home decoration mean dismantling an elaborate network of canes and foliage?

POSITIONING

Use the versatile qualities of plants to maximum effect in your home. A mixture of gentle greens will make a cosy sitting room even more relaxing. A dazzling flowering plant can make a strong visual point in a planned colour scheme. Any plant you like will give a lift to a dull corner, simply by virtue of being alive. Do not neglect the possibilities of lighting to emphasize leaves with interesting patterns or shapes. Use the floors as well as tables, windowsills, shelves and hanging containers to provide interest at different levels, and do not be frightened of experimenting. Only you know what your home has to offer, but the following suggestions may give some basic ideas about which plant can be grown where.

ABOVE: A trough full of brilliant Impatiens (busy Lizzie) brightens up a kitchen windowsill.
OPPOSITE: A tiered arrangement adds colour and interest to a small corner of an old cottage bathroom. Plants are chosen to provide contrast in shape, as well as colour and height: Philodendron Scandens, Saintpaulia, Ficus pumila, and Howea.

Windowsill:

Ananas
Azalea
Beloperone
Cacti and succulents
Chlorophytum
Chrysanthemum
Croton
Cyclamen
Hedera
Hibiscus
Hydrangea
Impatiens
Jasmine
Polyanthus
Tradescantia

Fireplace (inactive):
Araucaria
Aspidistra
Bromelaids
Dracaena marginata
Ferns
Gardenia
Howea
Monstera
Neanthe
Philodendron scandens
Phoenix
Rhoicissus rhomboidea

Hall: (poorly lit):
Aspidistra
Asplenium
Cissus antarctica
Dracaena marginata
Philodendron scandens
Rhoicissus rhomboidea

Hall (well lit):
Ananas
Chlorophytum
Dracaena deremensis
Ficus elastica
Hedera
Jasmine
Tradescantia

Kitchen:
Aphelandra
Begonia rex
Bromeliads
Columnea
Dracaena deremensis
Dracaena terminalis
Ferns
Fittonia
Gardenia
Hibiscus
Maranta
Palms
Saintpaulia
Stephanotis

Bathroom (heated):
Anthurium
Begonia rex
Bromeliads
Columnea
Dieffenbachia
Ferns
Fittonia
Ficus pumila
Gardenia
Hoya
Maranta
Palms
Philodendron scandens
Saintpaulia
Stephanotis

Room centres and shady corners:
Aspidistra
Bromeliads
Ferns
Ficus benjamina
Ficus pumila
Maranta
Palms
Philodendron scandens

ABOVE LEFT: *An old fireplace makes a perfect setting for an eye-catching display: Monstera, Cordyline terminalis and Rhoicissus rhomboidea (in copper pot); a trailing Hedera canariensis and Neoregelia carolinae 'Tricolor' (foreground).*
BELOW LEFT: *A grouped arrangement of trailing plants makes an effective table decoration.*
OPPOSITE: *In this living room, plants complement the patio outside, as well as the interior decor. A dramatic effect is created by positioning plants of various sizes at different levels in the room.*

FOLIAGE PLANTS

These indoor plants can provide colour and interest in your home all year round. Foliage plants offer an enormous range of appealing shapes and forms. Whether a houseplant is required to fill a large area, act as a screen, or simply provide subtle foliage, there will be one in this group to suit the purpose.

Foliage plants with plain green leaves will grow in shady corners. Those with coloured or variegated leaves need more light, but they should not be placed in direct sunlight.

Contrary to popular belief, foliage houseplants can provide some of the most brilliant and effective hues in the plant world; some of the colours even change according to the season. Because they come in so many shapes and sizes, these plants also offer plenty of scope for bowl arrangements, hanging baskets and other group displays.

Most foliage plants last a number of years before they either die or outgrow their situation, although many soon become part of the furnishings and in some cases, part of the family! Fortunately, the majority are far less trouble to maintain than other houseplants. Foliage plants may lack the impact of flowers or blossom, but they do provide an important, consistent, natural element within the home.

ANANAS*

The ananas or pineapple is a most interesting plant, grown for its attractive foliage. Two forms are available: the true pineapple, with its plain green leaves, which in the greenhouse can be induced to produce edible fruit; and the variegated form which produces a bright pink but inedible fruit.

The pointed strap-like leaves that radiate from the centre are covered on each edge with tiny barbs that tend to cling on to net curtains and snag careless fingers. They are certainly not suitable plants to grow with children about.

General Care: Ananas are hardy, and although they like a temperature of around 18°C (65°F) will tolerate a lower one, though not below 15°C (60°F). Let them dry out between waterings. A dry atmosphere is of no concern, nor indeed is direct sunlight; they seem to enjoy both.

If you have one that has not fruited, you can try a very simple method to initiate fruiting. Simply place a couple of ripe apples on a saucer next to the plant and cover up the saucer and plant with a polythene bag. Leave the plant and the apples under the bag for several days and then remove them. The gas given off by the apples, ethylene, should encourage the plant to fruit within three to four months. If it does not, try again.

Propagation: Propagation is best carried out by cutting off the rosette of leaves at the top of the fruit. Make the cut about 1 cm (½ inch) below the base of the rosette. Dip the cut end in hormone rooting powder and pot in a mixture of four parts seed compost to one part sand. Rooting may take about two months.

Pests and Diseases: The ananas is not prone to attack by many pests or diseases. The only problem may be mealy bugs which like to hide in the niche between the leaf stalks. Regular inspection and treatment will keep them at bay.

ARAUCARIA EXCELSA*

Better known as the Norfolk Island pine, *Araucaria excelsa* is a close relative of the Monkey Puzzle tree – the tall pine-like tree that is often seen in large gardens. The Norfolk Island pine is an elegant Christmas-tree-like houseplant that normally grows to between 1.5 and 2 metres (4 and 6½ ft) indoors. It is not hardy and must be grown indoors.

General Care: The adaptable araucaria tolerates a wide range of conditions. As an optimum, it prefers a temperature of 15-18°C (60-65°F) and a reasonably well-lit position, even in full sun. The plant can, however, be grown at lower temperatures down to 10°C (50°F) with more shade.

The one thing the araucaria does not like is too much water. Allow the compost to dry out between waterings. The soft spine-like foliage collects dust, which is best removed by rinsing the plant with tepid water – you could even give it a shower in the bath!

Araucaria excelsa, Aspidistra (back) and Ananas

Propagation: The only way to propagate araucaria is from seed, which should be sown in a half pot filled with seed compost. Lightly cover the seed with compost and keep at 20°C (68°F) until germinated. When the seedlings are large enough to handle – approximately 5 cm (2 inches) tall – gently prick them out and pot up singly in 9 cm (3½ inch) pots filled with potting compost.

Pests and Diseases: Though rarely troubled by pests araucaria may be attacked by mealy bugs and root mealy bugs.

ASPIDISTRA*

Although not a spectacular plant, aspidistra is extremely reliable. The dark green strap-like leaves are held erect by the plant, which needs a striking container to set it off.

General Care: The aspidistra does not demand a great deal of attention. A temperature of around 18°C (65°F) is ideal and a position away from the direct glare of the sun is most satisfactory. A dry environment may cause the leaf tips and edges to turn brown; if this occurs, try misting the leaves with tepid water. Clean the leaves, which tend to trap dust, by lightly wiping with a cotton wool pad moistened with water.

Allow the plant almost to dry out in between waterings. Do not overwater, particularly in winter.

Propagation: This is carried out by division of the roots in spring or summer.

Pests and Diseases: Watch for spider mites and mealy bugs.

BEGONIA REX**

The *Begonia rex* or 'fan plant' is available in a wide range of leaf colours and patterns. The leaves are roughly heart-shaped with prominent fleshy veins on the underside. The small, insignificant flowers may be pale pink or white.

General Care: *Begonia rex* likes a well-lit position away from the scorching rays of the sun. It is therefore best to place the plant on a windowsill peeping from behind a curtain or even up to a metre (3 ft) away from the window. Fortunately the plant is fairly tolerant of a warm dry environment and is usually happy at a temperature of about 18°C (65°F). Water regularly but in moderation; reduce the watering to a minimum in winter or the plant may rot.

Propagation: The method of propagation is by an extraordinary type of leaf cutting. Select a well-formed mature (not old) leaf, lay it face down and cut it into postage-stamp squares using a sharp knife. Lightly dip the underside of the leaf cuttings in hormone rooting powder and gently lay right-side up on the surface of a seed tray or half pot filled with moistened seed compost. Cover with a polythene bag and keep at about 21°C (70°F). Remove any cuttings that wither or rot; about half should 'take'. Remove the cover when the little plantlets start to grow from the cut edge of the pieces. When they are large enough to handle, gently prick them out and pot up singly in potting compost.

Pests and Diseases: *Begonia rex* sometimes suffers from mildew, a fungus that leaves a white deposit on the surface of the leaf, and mealy bugs. Occasionally botrytis (grey mould) will infect the plant, particularly under cool, dark growing conditions.

CHLOROPHYTUM*

The chlorophytum has long been known as the spider plant, and now it has also acquired the popular name St. Bernard Lily. It has green and white striped leaves and reproduces itself with cascades of flowering runners that carry small plantlets.

General Care: Chlorophytums are very easy to keep and adapt well to various household conditions. Lots of light and a temperature of about 15°C (60°F) is best but by no means essential.

In early spring, shade the plant from the first scorching rays of the sun as these can damage the leaves. The plant adapts rapidly, however, and can soon tolerate direct sunlight for periods of the day.

Avoid overwatering and allow the plant to become dry between waterings. Do not worry if the leaf tips turn brown, as they may well do. Simply snip off the browning tips with a pair of scissors.

Propagation: The plantlets on the chlorophytum's long hanging trails can easily be propagated, when large enough. Simply look for the start of the first roots which appear even before the plantlet is removed from its parent. When these are evident, cut the plantlet off from the trail and gently pot up in a 9 cm (3½ inch) pot of potting compost. Cut back the trail to the base of the parent to keep the original plant looking tidy.

Pests and Diseases: Aphids are normally the only problem, although older plants are sometimes affected by mealy bugs and root mealy bugs.

CISSUS ANTARCTICA*

Sometimes referred to as the kangaroo vine, the cissus has a very similar habit to the rhoicissus. The leaf shape is a pointed oval with a serrated but not at all sharp, edge. Indeed, the leaves are very soft and rather tender, although the plant itself is quite tough.

General Care: An indoor temperature of between 15-18°C (60-65°F) is best, although 13°C (55°F) is adequate. A reasonably light position is favoured. Too much direct sunlight will bleach the colour out of the leaves. Do not keep the plant in a dry atmosphere as dehydration causes leaf tips and edges to turn brown.

The cissus is a good climbing plant but it may become a little straggly. If this happens trim back to keep it in shape.

Propagation: Use stem cuttings produced when pruning the plant. Cut them into sections each with three or four leaves, retaining about 2.5 cm (1 inch) stem below the bottom leaf. Dip this end into hormone rooting powder and insert into potting compost. Several cuttings can go in one pot – about five to a 9 cm (3½ inch) pot is perfectly all right. Cover the cuttings with a polythene bag until they have rooted. Pot on as necessary.

Pests and Diseases: Mealy bugs and aphids may attack.

Chlorophytum, Cissus antarctica and Begonia rex (front)

CORDYLINE TERMINALIS***

Cordyline terminalis, the flaming dragon tree, takes its name from its beautifully coloured spear-shaped leaves of cerise-red to deep green.

General Care: This plant needs tender loving care if it is to thrive. It requires a near-constant temperature of 18-21°C (65-70°F) and a fairly high level of humidity, as the leaves tend to turn brown at the edges. Give it a lightly shaded position well away from draughts. In the summer, do not allow the compost to dry out; reduce watering to a minimum in winter.

Propagation: Suckers may appear in spring. Detach them carefully from the parent plant and plant each one in a 10 cm (4 inch) pot of John Innes No. 2 compost. It is also possible to propagate from stem cuttings if there are any available after pruning the plant to shape. Insert them deep in a mixture of equal parts peat and sand at 18-21°C (64-70°F) in a frame. When young growth can be seen, transfer the young plants to single pots of John Innes No. 2 potting compost and grow on.

Pests and Diseases: Red spider mites, mealy bugs and root mealy bugs are the main pests to watch out for; keep a close watch in spring and summer for aphids on young growth.

CROTON***

The correct botanical name for the croton, popularly known as Joseph's coat, is *Codiaeum*. It is a shrubby houseplant that is available in a variety of striking colours and leaf shapes.

General Care: Crotons love to bask in the sun. To obtain the most attractive colour in the leaves, expose the plant to as much sunlight as possible. You will find that the colours are at their best in summer; during the winter the plant turns a greener hue.

The croton is rather a delicate houseplant and is very sensitive to fluctuations in temperature. As temperature drops, so do the leaves as from a tree in autumn. Keep the plant at a near constant 18-20°C (65-68°F) particularly during the winter when it is at its most vulnerable. Allow it almost to dry out between waterings. Shaping can be achieved by light pruning.

If a strange spiky growth appears with starburst-like bobbles all over it, don't worry: these are the flowers, unimpressive though they are. Leave them until they have finished and then cut the spikes off.

Propagation: Crotons are not easy to propagate but if you want to try, take tip cuttings approximately 10 cm (4 inches) long. Dip into hormone rooting powder and insert into a 9 cm (3½ inch) pot of seed compost. Cover with a polythene bag and keep at 21°C (70°F) until rooted. Remove the bag and grow on in the pot. Pot on as necessary.

Pests and Diseases: Crotons are prone to red spider mites, mealy bugs and scale insects.

Dracaena deremensis and Dracaena marginata (front)

DIEFFENBACHIA**

The dieffenbachia, now commonly named leopard lily, used to be called dumb cane. It vaguely resembles a sugar cane plant but has highly variegated leaves and occasionally produces an insignificant flower spike that looks like an arum lily. The sap of the plant is poisonous and care should therefore be taken when trimming any leaves on the plant. Do not have one if there are children about.

General Care: Dieffenbachias like a warm, humid environment with a temperature of about 20°C (68°F). As they prefer light shade they are happiest in the middle of a room.

Though watering is not so critical, dieffenbachias are best kept relatively moist in summer, somewhat drier in winter. Yellowing leaves should be cut off at the base before they rot. If the plant becomes too tall with a long bare stem, cut it back to about 5 cm (2 inches) above soil level and it will break into growth again.

Propagation: Dieffenbachias sometimes produce side shoots which can be teased away from the parent plant and potted on. Alternatively, if you cut the plant back, divide the stem into 5 cm (2 inch) sections. Apply hormone rooting powder to one edge of each section and lay them with this side down in a tray of moist seed compost. Cover and keep at 21°C (70°F) until rooted. Remove the cover and allow to grow on until large enough to handle and pot up.

Pests and Diseases: Red spider mites and mealy bugs are the worst nuisance; root mealy bugs may inhibit growth.

Croton (front) and Dieffenbachia

DRACAENA*

Dracaena deremensis is one of the hardier species of this family. The leaf colour of the plant is attractive and the long slender pointed leaves are beautifully patterned in parallel streaks of green, white and cream. *Dracaena marginata* bears narrow dark green leaves radiating from the centre.

General Care: A slightly shaded situation is best, but short periods of exposure to sunlight will be tolerated. Let the compost dry out between waterings. Because of their thick leaves, dracaenas can store water for quite a long time and can cope with being kept on the dry side. A temperature of around 18°C (65°F) is best although plants will tolerate cooler conditions.

Propagation: Take stem cuttings and cut into pieces 2-3 cm (about 1 inch) long. Lay these sections on their side in a tray of seed compost. If kept at around 21°C (70°F) rooting should take place within eight weeks. Pot up when the young plants are large enough to handle and grow on.

Pests and Diseases: Mealy bugs and root mealy bugs are the major pests; the former may be found tucked in the little niche at the base of the leaf stalk where it joins the main stem. Occasionally the new leaves will stick together and the may mature satisfactorily. If not trim off the affected part.

FICUS BENJAMINA**

Ficus benjamina, weeping fig, is an elegant plant with cascading foliage that makes it particularly suitable as a single specimen plant rather than part of a group display.

General Care: The weeping fig is not as hardy as its sturdy relative, the rubber plant. Ideally, *Ficus benjamina* needs a stable temperature of around 20°C (68°F), although a steady 15°C (60°F) is adequate. The plant must be kept free from draughts. If it is subject to sudden 'chilling', premature leaf drop rapidly ensues, leaving the plant looking like a skeleton. Give weeping figs a situation of semi-shade a metre (3 ft) or so away from a window; direct sunlight may bleach the leaves. Allow the plant to dry out between waterings. A humid environment is beneficial but not essential.

Propagation: *Ficus benjamina* is very tricky to propagate. Those who are keen, however, should take tip cuttings about 7.5-10 cm (3-4 inches) in length, dip them in hormone rooting powder and insert individually in a 9 cm (3½ inch) pot filled with seed compost. Keep at 21°C (70°F) and cover with a polythene bag to conserve moisture. When rooted, pot on into John Innes No. 2 compost.

Pests and Diseases: Mealy bugs and scale insects are the most likely problems.

OPPOSITE: *Ficus elastica, Ficus benjamina and Ficus pumila (front)*

FICUS ELASTICA*

This must be the most common houseplant! The rubber plant, as it is familiarly known, has become amazingly popular. Its thick glossy green leaves grow alternately up the stem of the plant, borne erect when young, drooping as they get older. Variegated forms are available with pink or cream tints on the margin. New leaves form inside a rosy-pink protective sheath, which is discarded when the young leaf unfurls.

General Care: The rubber plant's reputation for durability has probably been overstated. Ideally, it should be grown in light shade at a temperature of about 18°C (65°F) away from draughts. Allow the compost to dry out between waterings; if it is kept too moist, the lower leaves may fall, giving you a metre (3 ft) of bare stem with two or three leaves at the top! To remove dust, clean the leaves with a cotton wool pad or soft cloth moistened with tepid water or a mixture of milk and water.

Propagation: Take stem cuttings in spring, making them 10-15 cm (4-6 inches) long. Insert in pots of equal parts peat and sand and maintain a temperature of 21-24°C (70-75°F) until rooted.

Leaf bud cuttings are used commercially for propagation, but results for the amateur are not always successful, so you are better off using stem cuttings.

Pests and Diseases: Mealy bugs and scale insects are the main pests to look out for, though aphids may disfigure young leaves.

FICUS PUMILA*

Commonly called the creeping fig, *Ficus pumila* is a little beauty. It has small green heart-shaped leaves, and a trailing or climbing habit. Its versatility as a houseplant is certain: it can be grown up a cane, trailing in a macramé hanging basket, in a bottle garden, or alone in an attractive container.

General Care: *Ficus pumila* is so easy to grow that every home should have one! A temperature of between 15-18°C (60-65°F) is acceptable – indeed it tolerates temperatures down to 10°C (50°F) without seeming to suffer.

Ficus pumila prefers a shady position and dislikes draughts although it is more durable than some plants. Do not allow the compost to dry out; once dehydrated, the creeping fig seldom revives. To remove dust from the leaves, rinse them with tepid water. Never apply leaf-shine preparations.

If growth becomes straggly, snip the plant into shape with sharp scissors and use the cuttings to propagate.

Propagation: Take stem cuttings about 7.5 cm (3 inches) long, dip them into hormone rooting powder and insert in 9 cm (3½ inch) pots of seed compost, putting about five cuttings to a pot. Cover with a polythene bag and keep at about 18°C (65°F) until rooted. Remove the polythene bag and grow on. Results are usually good.

Pests and Diseases: Aphids sometimes attack the young growth in spring and summer. Mealy bugs and root mealy bugs may be a problem.

leaves dehydrate. It needs a temperature of about 20°C (68°F). Aim to keep the compost relatively moist.

Propagation: When growth becomes leggy, trim off straggling shoots to make the plant a better balanced shape. Insert the cuttings in hormone rooting powder and plant five to a 9 cm (3½ inch) pot of seed compost. Keep at about 21°C (70°F) and cover with a polythene bag to reduce water loss from the leaves. When the cuttings have rooted, remove the bag and grow on.

Pests and Diseases: Although rarely attacked by pests, this plant occasionally suffers from root mealy bugs.

FITTONIA ARGYRONEURA*

Perhaps better known as the little snakeskin plant or mini-fittonia, this pretty little specimen is delicately patterned in green with white veins. It is a low-growing plant, good for ground cover in mixed plantings or bottle gardens.

General Care: If there is one thing the mini-fittonia dislikes, apart from the cold, it is being allowed to dry out. Once it starts to wilt its chances of recovery are slim. Keep it moist most of the time, at a temperature of about 18°C (65°F) in a well-lit situation away from direct sunlight. Avoid draughts and a dry environment. Trim as necessary to maintain a compact plant during growth.

Propagation: The method of propagation is easy and usually successful. When the plant becomes rather leggy, cut off the straggling shoots, dip them in hormone rooting powder and insert five in a 9 cm (3½ inch) pot of seed compost. Cover with a polythene bag until they have rooted. Remove the bag and let the plants grow on.

Pests and Diseases: Fortunately, the mini-fittonia is rarely affected by pests.

FITTONIA VERSCHAFFELTII***

The larger leaved fittonia, or snakeskin plant, has leaves of deep green with rosy pink veins. It grows very close to the surface of the pot and makes a useful background plant for bottle gardens and plant arrangements.

General Care: Surprisingly, it is this, the larger leaved variety of fittonia, that is the more delicate. It prefers a slightly shaded position away from direct sunlight, such as in the middle of a room, well away from draughts. It is very susceptible to a dry environment: without high humidity the

HEDERA CANARIENSIS*

Hedera canariensis, the Canary Island ivy, is a magnificent species with large variegated leaves of deep green and cream.

General Care: The Canary Island ivy likes sun or shade but dislikes being kept too warm. Keep it where the temperature will not exceed 20°C (68°F). In rooms warmer than this, the atmosphere is likely to be too dry and the leaf tips and edges will turn brown. In winter, the variegation tends to fade a little, but once light intensities increase in spring, the brighter pigments return.

Like all ivies, *Hedera canariensis* is a good climber or trailer, but to climb will need the support of a frame, trellis or cane. It is a useful plant for a porch or unheated conservatory. Take care not to overwater this ivy, but let the compost become somewhat dry between waterings.

LEFT: Fittonia argyroneura, and the larger-leafed Fittonia verschaffeltii
RIGHT: Hedera helix and Hedera canariensis

Propagation: Simply trim off any unwanted stems and cut them into pieces with about three leaves on each. Leave about 2.5 cm (1 inch) of stem below the bottom leaf. Dip the cuttings in hormone rooting powder and insert them five to a 9 cm (3½ inch) pot of seed compost. Cover with a polythene bag to conserve moisture during rooting and remove the bag as soon as the plants start to grow.

Pests and Diseases: Scale insects can cause severe damage by mottling the leaves. Aphids, mealy bugs and root mealy bugs can also be a problem.

HEDERA HELIX*

The small-leaved English ivy produces an attractive climbing or trailing plant that can be grown outdoors as well as indoors. There are many variations with leaves of different shape, size and colour.

General Care: None of the ivies likes to be too warm. They prefer cool, even cold, light airy conditions, and are particularly happy in an unheated porch or conservatory. In a warm, dry environment the leaves will dehydrate and eventually die. A temperature between 7-10°C (45-50°F) is adequate. Take care with watering, and allow compost to become almost dry before rewatering. Most ivies that die have been overwatered.

Don't worry if any variegation fades in winter; in the spring, as light intensities increase, it will return. Trimming of wayward growth can be done at any time to keep the plant in shape. If the plant begins to outgrow its home, you can always plant it outside, providing you harden it off first. Spring or early summer is probably the best time to do this.

Propagation: When you trim the ivy, cut the stems into pieces with three or four leaves, leaving about 2.5 cm (1 inch) of stem below the bottom leaf. Make sure that you don't get them the wrong way round – it's easy to do! Dip the bottom piece of stem in hormone rooting powder and insert five to seven cuttings in a 9 cm (3½ inch) pot of seed compost. Cover with a polythene bag until the cuttings have rooted. Remove the bag and grow on in the same pot.

Pests and Diseases: If ivies should become infested with aphids, red spider mites or mealy bugs take speedy remedial action. Leaf spot disease may occur on weak plants.

MARANTA LEUCONEURA 'KERCHOVEANA'***

The little maranta, sometimes called rabbit's tracks because of the brown blotches on the oval green leaves, is more commonly known as the prayer plant because of its nightly habit of raising its leaves together like praying hands. Marantas produce tiny, violet-pink flowers on a long slender stalk.

General Care: Marantas are difficult to grow. They like warm, humid conditions in semi-shade with a steady temperature of about 20°C (68°F). The leaves will wither in a dry environment. Probably the best way to grow the plant is in a bottle garden: it will then be protected from draughts, enjoy high humidity and be rooted in a moist compost. Give marantas a liquid feed every two weeks from April to September.

Propagation: Division of the main plant is recommended. Alternatively, take tip cuttings from straggly growth if it occurs. Insert the cuttings in pots of equal parts peat and sand and maintain a temperature of 21°C (70°F). Apply a fine mist of tepid water daily. When established pot on into larger pots of John Innes No.2 potting compost.

Pests and Diseases: Marantas are occasionally troubled by red spider mites, mealy bugs and root mealy bugs.

MARANTA TRICOLOUR***

Maranta tricolour which you may also find as *Maranta leuconeura* 'erythrophylla' has the common name of red herringbone. It has exquisitely patterned leaves, oval in shape, dark green in colour, with well-defined deep rose veins and ribs.

General Care: Like all marantas, the red herringbone is choosy about its conditions. It needs high humidity and a temperature of about 20°C (68°F) in a slightly shaded situation. It prefers to be kept relatively moist at the roots and is happiest in a bottle garden or arranged in a group with other plants. Tiny violet-pink flowers are sometimes produced on slender stalks during spring and summer.

Propagation: Propagate by division or by stem cuttings. These should be taken from top growth and have two or three leaves attached. Insert each stem in a 9 cm (3½ inch) pot of equal parts peat and sand and keep constantly moist at 21°C (70°F) until rooted. Pot on into larger containers of John Innes No.2 potting compost.

Pests and Diseases: This plant is occasionally attacked by red spider mites, mealy bugs and root mealy bugs.

MONSTERA DELICIOSA*

Sometimes called Swiss cheese plant or Mexican breadfruit plant, the monstera is an unusual species with slits and holes in its large glossy green leaves. It may reach 2 metres (6 ft) or more in height, but in the home it is normally about half this height. Its tentacle-like aerial roots are an unusual feature.

General Care: Monsteras adapt to most environments with little trouble. To get the best out of the plant, ensure that it enjoys a semi-shaded position where the atmosphere is relatively humid, as these two factors are important if the plant is to produce leaves of characteristic shape. In a bright, dry position it will revert to a smaller leaf without slits or holes. To remove dust, clean leaves occasionally with a cotton wool pad moistened with tepid water or milk and

water. Proprietary leafshine materials may damage leaves.

If the aerial roots become too rampant, wind them around the plant to encourage them to grow back into the compost, or put them into damp sphagnum moss or moss peat. All monsteras over 30 cm (12 inches) high need the support of a stake, and a 'moss pole' is ideal.

Monstera deliciosa, Maranta 'Tricolour', Maranta leuconeura kerchoveana (front) and Peperomia magnoliaefolia (front)

Propagation: Monstera may produce a side shoot that can be teased away when it is 15 cm (6 inches) tall and potted in John Innes No. 3 potting compost.
Pests and Diseases: Monsteras are generally free from pests.

PEPEROMIA MAGNOLIAEFOLIA*

Commonly known as the desert privet, *Peperomia magnoliaefolia* is a most attractive plant with almost circular, waxy succulent leaves that are variegated green and cream.

General Care: The desert privet is exceptionally adaptable and is ideal for a beginner's collection. It will continue to thrive in a wide temperature range of 10-18°C(50-65°F). Light is important as it keeps the variegated colours bright. In a shady position the leaves will become dull and the variegation will fade.

As the thick fleshy leaves act as water storage reservoirs, it is advisable to keep the compost rather dry. Too much water will drown the roots and the plant will rot. Let the compost almost dry out between waterings.

Propagation: This is best achieved by rooting stem cuttings. When the plant becomes rather leggy and top-heavy, cut it back to a more compact shape. Trim each cutting to a section about 5-7.5 cm (2-3 inches) long. Dip in hormone rooting powder and insert three cuttings into a 9 cm (3½ inch) pot of moist seed compost. Do not cover with polythene, as the leaves can store enough water to stop the plant wilting and could rot if kept in a damp, humid environment.

Pests and Diseases: Aphids and red spider mites sometimes attack the desert privet in spring and summer. Take prompt action to stop any damage, otherwise the plant will be disfigured.

PHILODENDRON SCANDENS*

The heart-shaped leaves of *Philodendron scandens* have given it the appropriate popular name of sweetheart plant. These handsome plain green leaves and a climbing habit make it a good-looking specimen plant or background feature in mixed arrangements. It normally requires some form of support, but can be treated as a trailer.

General Care: A semi-shaded position away from direct sunlight is ideal with a temperature of about 18°C (65°F). The plant should be allowed almost to dry out between waterings; keep watering to a minimum in winter.

As the plant grows, it may become untidy. If so, cut back to maintain its shape, and use the trimmings to provide cuttings.

Propagation: Take stem cuttings with one leaf each and about 2.5 cm (1 inch) of stem above and below. If the tip of the shoot is used, make sure it has one mature leaf and about 2.5 cm (1 inch) of stem below it. Make sure you keep the stem cuttings the right way round. If it helps, reduce the length of stem above the leaf slightly so that you can see the difference. Dip the cuttings into hormone rooting powder and insert between three and five in a 9 cm (3½ inch) pot of peat-based seed compost. Cover tightly with a polythene bag. When rooted, remove the bag and leave to grow on, potting on the plants together as they mature.

Pests and Diseases: The sweetheart plant is generally free of pests.

RHOICISSUS RHOMBOIDEA*

The *Rhoicissus rhomboidea* or grape ivy is an accommodating climbing plant with shiny green leaves of serrated diamond shape. These leaves are produced in groups of three on long stems which climb by using tendrils.

The grape ivy can be trained up a single trellis or support to grow about 1 metre (3 ft) tall.

General Care: Rhoicissus prefers a slightly shaded position away from sunlight – it is ideal for a shady corner. If the plant receives too much light the leaves will turn from a deep green to an unattractive yellow-green.

Rhoicissus will happily grow at temperatures between 15-18°C (60-65°F). A dry atmosphere may cause dehydration of the leaves but this can be avoided by keeping the plant at a slightly lower temperature. Allow the compost to become almost dry before rewatering; do not overwater. Prune to tidy the shape of the plant if necessary in late winter.

Propagation: Use prunings as stem and tip cuttings. Trim each one to give about 2.5 cm (1 inch) of stem below the bottom of three leaves. Dip the end into hormone rooting powder. Insert five to seven cuttings in a 9 cm (3½ inch) pot, using a peat-based potting compost or John Innes No. 1 potting compost. Cover with a polythene bag to keep them moist. Once they have rooted, remove the bag and allow the plants to grow on.

Pests and Diseases: Rhoicissus are rarely attacked by pests or diseases.

TRADESCANTIA*

Tradescantia is one of those few plants so popular that it is as well known by its proper name as by any of the common names that have been attached to it. An attractive trailing plant, it looks best in small hanging baskets, high on a shelf or in a pot fixed to the wall.

General Care: Tradescantias are most adaptable plants. They grow well in various environments, but are best in a well-lit position at a temperature between 10-15°C (50-60°F). Allow the compost to dry out between waterings. Trim the plant back when it looks straggly and bare stems are visible.

Propagation: Take cuttings from leading shoots, reducing them to about 5 cm (2 inches) in length. Insert between three and five of these cuttings in a 9 cm (3½ inch) pot filled with potting compost and keep moist, but not wet. Rooting is rapid; during spring and summer it may take only two or three weeks. Once rooted, grow on in the same pot.

Pests and Diseases: Tradescantias are generally free of pests.

OPPOSITE: Philodendron scandens, Rhoiscissus rhomboidea and Tradescantia (front)

PALMS & FERNS

These are two distinctive groups of plants offering variety in shape and form to any houseplant collection. Ferns are particularly valuable because they will grow in positions other plants could not tolerate.

Ferns will thrive in shady positions, providing they are kept moist. Their natural habitat is the tropical rain forest floor where humidity is high, but light intensity is low because of the tremendous canopy of leaves provided by taller plants.

Ferns vary in their temperature requirements but they must have plenty of moisture, and not only in the soil. A humid atmosphere is important and ferns will normally only grow successfully in a centrally heated home if humidifiers are present. The bathroom is often the most suitable room in the house to grown ferns in.

Although generally more expensive than ferns, palms are well worth growing because they are long-lived and not difficult to grow. Palms are not so exacting in their moisture, light or soil requirements, but they must have a minimum winter temperature of 10°C (50°F). These plants are an excellent investment for they are slow growing and given time they will develop into tall, elegant specimens.

Apart from filling awkward spaces, palms and ferns provide delicate foliage and soft green hues amongst the harsher outlines of many home furnishings.

ADIANTUM**

The best-known variety is *Adiantum capillus-veneris*, commonly known as maidenhair, which is one of the most popular ferns. Its delicate fronds, rosy pink when young, mature to a fresh bright green.

General Care: The maidenhair fern requires a humid environment. It will grow well in cool temperatures – as low as 10°C (50°F), but its optimum temperature is 18°C (65°F). It needs a situation well away from direct sunlight. Make sure that the compost never dries out. If this happens, and the plant looks as if dehydration has killed it, don't give up. Provided it has not been allowed to stay dry for too long, it is possible to rejuvenate the plant. Cut off the dead fronds about ½ cm (¼ inch) above soil level and carefully water the plant over the next few weeks. With a certain amount of luck, the plant will eventually produce fresh growth and regain its former glory.

Propagation: Adiantum can be propagated from spores in the same way as other ferns (see Asplenum – opposite). However, Adiantum is a fairly delicate plant and therefore difficult to grow successfully from spores.

Pests and Diseases: These are not a problem for adiantum.

ASPARAGUS FERN*

Not all types of asparagus are grown to be eaten! Of the ornamental varieties suited to pot culture two make excellent houseplants, *Asparagus plumosus* and *Asparagus sprengeri*. They produce beautiful bright green feathery foliage which is, incidentally, invaluable in flower arrangements. They are displayed to good advantage in a hanging basket or on a high shelf.

General Care: Although asparagus ferns prefer not to be allowed to dry out completely, they can tolerate this condition even in summer. Nevertheless, the compost is best kept relatively moist through the growing season, and drier in winter. A lightly shaded situation is best, although they will tolerate direct light or deeper shade.

During the growing season, provide a temperature of around 13-18°C (55-65°F). A minimum temperature of about 10°C (45°F) is required in winter.

Propagation: Propagate by division in spring. Water the plant well first to ease separation. Gently tease the roots apart using a sharp knife to cut cleanly through any parts that do not separate easily. Pot up each piece into a suitably sized pot containing John Innes No.2 potting compost and grow on.

Pests and Diseases: Asparagus ferns grown in the home are generally trouble-free, but look out for scale insects.

Asplenium, Howea (see page 46) and Adiantum

ASPLENIUM*

Asplenium nidus or bird's-nest fern has broad, strap-like fronds radiating from a central rosette.

General Care: One of the easiest ferns to grow, the bird's nest fern is quite happy at relatively low temperatures down to 10°C (50°F) although it prefers to be kept at around 18°C (65°F). It is also rather more tolerant than other ferns of a dry atmosphere, although it shares with them a preference for semi-shade, away from the scorching rays of direct sunlight. Watering is not really a problem as the asplenium is less susceptible than many other ferns to over- or underwatering.

Propagation: The asplenium can be propagated from minute dust-like spores produced from dark brown-coloured gill-like objects on the underside of mature fronds. Collect these spores carefully and sprinkle them on to the surface of a half pot filled with a mixture of peat and loam-based seed compost (1:1 ratio), or a peat-based seed compost. Place the pot in a polythene bag and keep moist at about 21°C (70°F) until the spores germinate. Leave until large enough to handle, then prick out and pot on.

Pests and Diseases: Scale insects are the most likely pests.

CHAMAEDOREA ELEGANS**

Also called *Neanthe bella* or parlour palm, this is a compact palm that takes some time to reach 60 cm (2 ft) in height and rarely grows taller. It is one of the easiest palms to cultivate.

General Care: Parlour palms prefer a semi-shaded position away from direct light which turns the leaves pale. Maintain a temperature of about 18°C (65°F) in spring and summer and spray once or twice a day with a mist of tepid water to increase humidity. In winter this palm prefers to be kept cooler, at 7-10°C (45-50°F). Let the compost get dry between waterings. Feed about once a month during the growing period (April-September).

Chamaedoreas sometimes produce a flower spike, which can be snipped off if you do not like the look of it. The flowers that form look like small yellow blobs. If you are lucky, tiny pea-like fruits may set, and these can be used for propagation. Flowers are unlikely to appear before the plant is three or four years old.

Propagation: You can buy seeds or save your own if you have a plant that flowers. Sow in a half pot filled with seed compost and then cover with a polythene bag. The seeds need a temperature of about 21°C (70°F) to germinate and even then they may take from three to six months to grow.

Pests and Diseases: Chamaedoreas are generally free of pests. Red spider mites, mealy bugs, root mealy bugs and scale insects are occasional problems, red spider mites being the most damaging to these plants.

CYCAS REVOLUTA*

This plant is more often referred to as the cycas palm or sago palm. The dark green leaves radiating from its centre give the plant a rosette-like form. It is similar to the phoenix (page 48), but much more rigid and compact.

General Care: Cycas are relatively slow growing. Because they are tolerant of conditions that true palms would find inhospitable they are relatively easy to care for. A temperature of about 18-20°C (65-68°F) is ideal with a moderate level of humidity, but the plant will tolerate a drier atmosphere and lower temperatures. The cycas will also adapt to varying light conditions from reasonably well lit areas to deep shade, although it prefers a semi-shaded position. Both during the summer growing season and the near-dormant winter period, cycas should be watered moderately and allowed to dry out between waterings.

Propagation: Cycas can be grown from seed; each one is 4 cm (1½ inches) long. You can obtain seeds from specialist producers and will find it interesting to germinate them. Each seed is protected by a woody shell similar to a hazelnut, but thicker. The shell should be carefully removed from the kernel by gently inserting the point of a penknife and levering it apart. Take great care not to cut your fingers or damage the kernel.

Bury the seed in a 9 cm (3½ inch) pot of seed compost. Cover and keep at around 24-27°C (75-80°F) until germinated. Bring into the light in a protected spot to grow on. Keep in the pot until it starts to outgrow it. Transplant into a 13 cm (5 inch) pot; you won't need to do this for a year or so.

Pests and Diseases: Cycas are sometimes attacked by mealy bugs and root mealy bugs.

HOWEA**

The *Howea forsteriana* commonly called the kentia palm is one of the most elegant palms with leathery leaves and usually grows to about 2 metres (6 ft) in height.

General Care: The kentia palm prefers a shady position away from draughts in a temperature of 13-18°C (55-65°F). Humidity and ventilation are important; in a stuffy dry environment the fronds will dehydrate and the edges turn brown. Although these can be trimmed off this is only a cosmetic treatment. Some move must be made to increase the humidity, such as spraying the plant with a mist of tepid water twice a day. Do not be tempted to treat the fronds with a leaf-shine cleaning material as this can often cause serious damage. Instead, simply wipe dust from the fronds with a cotton wool pad or soft cloth moistened with tepid water or a mixture of milk and water.

Propagation: It is difficult to propagate palms from seed but possible – with patience. Germination is slow and erratic and may take from three to six months. Sow the seeds in a half pot of seed compost. Lightly cover and keep in a polythene bag at about 21°C (70°F). When the seeds have germinated, pot them on.

Pests and Diseases: Howeas are generally trouble-free.

NEPHROLEPIS EXALTATA**

The nephrolepis or ladder fern is one of the most common and popular ferns grown. It has long, stately fronds of pale or bright green depending on variety and looks especially attractive on an old-fashioned plant stand, or in a hanging basket.

General Care: Nephrolepis prefer a semi-lit situation away from direct sunlight. A temperature of about 18°C (65°F) is ideal provided that the atmosphere is not too dry, for its thin fronds are susceptible to dehydration. Nephrolepis will, however, tolerate a minimum winter temperature of 10°C (50°F). Do not let the compost dry out as this can at worst cause the plant to die back, at the least exacerbate the problem of drying fronds. An acid compost is required, and feeding every two weeks from mid-summer will give a good growth of fronds.

Propagation: Nephrolepis can be propagated from spores but it is easier to increase by using runners growing from the top of the rhizome. The runners should be potted in a moist peaty compost in late spring or summer. They will root quickly if kept moist and warm.

Pests and Diseases: Fortunately the nephrolepis is rarely troubled by pests. Physiological disorders associated with the wrong environment are likely to be the only problem.

Chamaedorea elegans and Nephrolepis exaltata (front)

Pellaea rotundiflora (back) and Platycerium bifurcatum (front)

PELLAEA ROTUNDIFOLIA**

The fronds of the diminutive pellaea or button fern are composed of small circular leaves. Fronds up to 50 cm (20 inches) long form a low spreading mat as the fern grows. Pellaeas can be most effective in small hanging baskets.

General Care: Unlike most ferns, the pellaea is happy in a light environment, though not direct sunlight. It will grow well under the low intensity of fluorescent lighting. The pellaea ideally likes a temperature of about 18°C (65°F) and needs to be kept reasonably moist. It will not tolerate temperatures below 7°C (45°F).

Propagation: Like other ferns, propagation from spores is the usual method (see Asplenium – page 45).

Pests and Diseases: Pellaeas are not usually troubled by pests or diseases.

PHOENIX CANARIENSIS*

Phoenix canariensis, sometimes called the date palm, is a magnificent plant of superb geometric form with gently cascading fronds radiating from the centre. It tends to grow about 2 metres (6 ft) high eventually in the home, although as it is slow growing, most specimens are less than 1 metre (3 ft).

General Care: The thin fronds of the date palm make it susceptible to dehydration in a warm, dry environment, which causes the tips and edges to turn brown. Increase the level of humidity around the plant by spraying it once or twice a day with a fine mist of tepid water. Watering should be carried out when the compost gets dry. Do not overwater. A temperature of about 18°C (65°F) is ideal, but the date palm will tolerate 10°C (50°F). Place the palm in the centre of the room away from direct light in order to provide the lightly shaded situation it prefers.

Propagation: Phoenix palms can be propagated from seed (date stones) germinated in a half pot filled with seed compost, enclosed in a polythene bag and kept at about 21°C (70°F). They will take about three to six months to germinate. The individual seedlings can then be potted up singly in John Innes No.1 potting compost.

Pests and Diseases: The stems and leaves may occasionally be attacked by red spider mites, mealy bugs, root mealy bugs and scale insects.

PLATYCERIUM BIFURCATUM*

The platycerium or stag's horn fern is a most extraordinary plant. It produces two totally different frond shapes: one the antler-like green frond that gives the plant its name and is produced in number, the other, the simple basal frond from which the green fronds emerge and which helps to secure the plant to its location. In the wild this location is the branch of a tree, for the platycerium is a tree-living fern.

General Care: Platyceriums are fairly tough plants and quite content at a temperature of about 15°C (60°F), although they are happiest at about 18°C (65°F). Allow the compost almost, but not quite, to dry out between waterings. Take care not to overwater. Give the plant a lightly shaded situation away from direct sunlight. It can be grown in a hanging basket or in a piece of cork bark filled with a mixture of sphagnum moss, potting compost and peat in equal proportions.

Propagation: The stag's horn fern can be propagated from spores produced from velvety brown patches, that appear on the underside of the frond tips. Collect the spores carefully and sprinkle lightly on the surface of a half pot filled with a mixture of equal parts peat and loam-based seed compost, or in a peat-based seed compost. Enclose the pot within a polythene bag and keep moist at a temperature of about 21°C (70°F). When the spores have germinated and are large enough to handle, pot up singly.

Pests and Diseases: Watch out for scale insects, the only likely pest.

PTERIS ENSIFORMIS 'VICTORIAE'**

This little fern with its beautifully slender dark green and white fronds, though not the easiest of ferns to grow, is so attractive that it is worth a little extra care.

General Care: Pteris are extremely susceptible to dehydration. They must be kept in humid conditions; occasional spraying with a fine mist of tepid water helps, but does not completely overcome the problem. It prefers a temperature of around 20°C (68°F) but in common with other ferns prefers a semi-shaded position away from direct sunlight. The minimum temperature it will tolerate is 10°C (50°F). *Pteris ensiformis* is useful for a bottle garden.

Phoenix canariensis

Propagation: Pteris spores can be germinated in the same way as other ferns, but propagation is not easy, and requires patience. (See Asplenum – page 45.)

Pests and Diseases: The plant is not likely to be troubled by any pests or diseases, which somewhat makes up for its rather exacting cultural requirements.

FLOWERING PLANTS

Unlike foliage plants, flowering houseplants provide a brilliant burst of colour in the home. They will remain in bloom for several weeks at least. Most flowering plants are best treated as a long-lasting bunch of flowers, rather than as a permanent display. Some, however, can be encouraged to flower for most of the year, with correct feeding.

Plants which remain in flower for several months, such as chrysanthemums, impatiens, saintpaulias and streptocarpus, are particularly valuable, providing colourful blooms when cut flowers are expensive.

Flowering plants require rather more care than most foliage ones. Light is an important factor. With the notable exception of saintpaulias, they need a well lit situation to flower successfully. A moist atmosphere is also essential. It is most crucial when the flower buds are forming. Spraying or misting frequently at this time will help to prevent buds dropping before they open.

Remove flower heads complete with stems as soon as they die, to keep the plant tidy and to avoid diseases encouraged by dead flowers. Most perennial flowering plants will flower the following year, providing they are not neglected after flowering.

ACHIMENES *

The achimenes is often called the 'hot water plant'. Although diminutive in height, reaching only about 20 cm (8 inches), it is usually a mass of flowers throughout the spring and summer in various shades of white, pink, purple and blue. The delicate-looking foliage is usually deep green. You can allow the growth to trail, or if you want a bushy, upright plant, three or four short canes or twigs will provide the necessary support.

General Care: Since achimenes like plenty of light they are well suited to being grown on a windowsill as long as it is not too warm. A temperature of around 18-20°C (65-68°F) is ideal during the growing season.

Although achimenes should not be allowed to dry out in spring and summer, avoid overwatering. Occasional feeding with diluted tomato fertilizer will help to maintain a well-formed and freely flowering plant right through the season, until September when it will start to fade. From September or October, reduce watering so that the compost gradually dries out, allowing the plant to die back to its root, or rather rhizome. It should then be stored in a dry, cool but frost-free place until spring when growth can be restored. It is common practice to submerge the pot in a bowl of warm, but not hot, water to break the plant's dormancy – hence the origin of its popular name.

Propagation: Achimenes are generally propagated from little rhizomes produced by each plant during the growing season. In spring, divide these up and plant them six to a 13 cm (5 inch) pot filled with peat-based compost. Maintain a temperature of about 16°C (61°F) and keep just moist, increasing the quantity of water gradually as growth appears.

Pests and Diseases: Aphids may occasionally be a problem on this plant.

AMARYLLIS*

For most of the year, the amaryllis or hippeastrum has little to show other than its broad strap-like leaves. When it flowers, however, the display is dramatic. Each bulb produces one or more magnificent blooms that are especially welcome in the drab months of late winter when prepared bulbs are usually brought into flower. The natural flowering time is spring. The flowers produced on 60 cm (2 ft) stems can be more than 10 cm (4 inches) across and vary in colour from white to pink and deep red.

General Care: Plant the amaryllis bulb in a 13-18 cm (5-7 inch) pot of John Innes No. 2 potting compost, leaving about one half of the bulb proud of the compost. In winter, give the plant as much light as possible and water moderately, but regularly. Give a weekly liquid feed and keep the plant warm, at around 18-20°C (65-68°F). Increase watering as the plant grows and eventually flowers.

After flowering, the leaves will grow more actively and the plant should continue to be fed at reduced strength. This will help to promote flower production for the following year. As the leaves start to wither, reduce watering and allow the plant to rest in a dry state for its dormant period during the autumn and early winter before starting into growth again in late winter or early spring.

Propagation: Either offsets or seed can be used. Separate offsets from the main plant when starting it into growth and pot up singly into 9 cm (3½ inch) pots, transferring them to the final pot as the roots expand.

Sow seed in half pots of seed compost in spring or summer, cover and keep at about 21°C (70°F). When they have germinated and are large enough to handle, prick them out, pot up separately and treat in the same way as offsets, although they will take at least three years to flower. Although bulb offsets are produced less freely than seeds they will flower sooner.

Pests and Diseases: Occasionally amaryllis may be attacked by mealy bugs.

ANTHURIUM**

The anthurium, or flamingo flower, is an unusual plant which produces colourful spathes that look like exotic flowers. The two most commonly grown varieties are *Anthurium andreanum,* which has a shield-shaped 'flower' of white, pink or brilliant red from which a finger-like stalk protrudes, and *Anthurium scherzerianum* which has an orange-red 'flower' and a curious piglet's-tail protuberance. The 'stalk' of one and the piglet's tail of the other are in fact the flowers.

General Care: The flamingo flower needs a fair amount of care and attention. It prefers a temperature of 18-21°C (65-70°F) and humid conditions. While it does not like too much direct sunlight, it will not thrive in too much shade. A well-lit position where the temperature is reasonably constant will provide a useful growing situation.

Amaryllis

Do not let the plant dry out, especially during the growing season. Mist regularly with tepid water. Feed it once a month from April to September with a tomato fertilizer applied at half strength.

The flowers, which appear throughout the year, can be used in cut flower arrangements where they may live for three or four weeks or more. If they are left on the plant, however, they may last for up to eight weeks, providing a brilliant display of colour.

Propagation: Sometimes the plant will produce a young one at its side. This can be separated when it is about 15 cm (6 inches) tall and potted up individually in a mixture of equal parts potting compost and moss peat.

Alternatively, anthuriums can be raised from seed produced from the true flowers, which swell up and yield the seed. These should be sown in half pots of seed compost and lightly covered. To germinate, keep the pots at 21°C (70°F) and enclosed in a polythene bag to conserve water and heat. When large enough to handle they can be transplanted and potted up singly.

Pests and Diseases: Anthuriums very rarely suffer from pests, although mealy bugs can sometimes be a nuisance and aphids occasionally attack young leaves and flowers.

Anthurium (page 51) and Aphelandra (front)

APHELANDRA***

The aphelandra, or zebra plant, bears a cone of bright golden-yellow flowers on a flower spike rising from luxurious leathery green leaves with white veins. The flowers last several weeks before they eventually fade and fall off. The plant can be persuaded to flower again the next year.

General Care: The aphelandra likes lots of light. Avoid draughts and aim for a temperature of about 18°C (65°F). The aphelandra likes water and will suffer if left to dry out. Once the plant has flowered, it tends to produce rather straggly growth. This can be controlled a little by careful pruning and by feeding with half-strength tomato fertilizer. Spring pruning, cutting back after flowering to above the last pair of leaves, will encourage a good shape and improve the chances of flowering again.

Propagation: When you prune the plant back in spring, use the prunings as cutting material. Cut up the stem, leaving about 5 cm (2 inches) below each pair of leaves. Dip each cutting in hormone rooting powder and insert singly in 9 cm (3½ inch) pots of John Innes No. 2 potting compost. Cover with polythene bags and keep them at a temperature of 21°C (70°F) until rooted. Grow on and eventually pot up into 13 cm (5 inch) pots to grow to maturity.

Pests and Diseases: Scale insects on the undersides of the leaves and on the stems are the worst nuisance to aphelandras. Aphids attack the young leaves and flowers in spring and summer.

AZALEA**

Rhododendron indicum, the Indian azalea, is a most colourful flowering plant that is seasonal from autumn to spring and is particularly popular at Christmas.

Azaleas are available in a wide range of colours from white, rose-pink and salmon to cerise-red. If looked after reasonably well, they will last in flower for up to eight weeks.

General Care: Keep azaleas reasonably moist. Watering is critical, and is best achieved by placing the plant in a bowl of tepid water, carefully submerging the root ball. When the plant has finished bubbling, remove it, let the surplus water drain away, and place it back in its saucer. Azaleas that are allowed to get dry seldom recover from the shock and rapidly decline.

Temperature and light are equally important. Keep the plant in a light and airy situation – a bedroom windowsill at about 15°C (60°F) is ideal. Central heating can often be fatal and will certainly reduce the flowering period to as little as two weeks.

When the plant has finished flowering it can be placed out of doors from May until September. Plunge the pot in a peat bed and keep it moist throughout the summer. Feeding with a tomato fertilizer at about half strength once a month will assist growth. One or two applications of Sequestrene will prevent yellowing of the leaves. When they have been brought back indoors in September, most azaleas will flower reasonably well.

Azalea – the reddish pink and pink-white types

They can be made to flower in greater profusion by a simple technique. In the evening, spray the plant with tepid water and place it in an airing cupboard overnight. Repeat this for a few weeks and you will find that the relatively high temperature and humidity have helped to produce flowers. Do remember to place the plant in full light during daylight hours.

Propagation: Azaleas can sometimes be raised from cuttings or seed but the results are usually so disappointing that it is not worth trying.

Pests and Diseases: Azaleas suffer from few pests although aphids can sometimes be a problem on the flower buds.

BELOPERONE GUTTATA**

The beloperone is more commonly known as the shrimp plant because of the oddly shaped shrimplike flowers it produces. They are small and white, enclosed in reddish-brown bracts, and last several weeks before dropping off.

General Care: Since the beloperone likes plenty of light, put the pot in a well-lit window. During the winter months, the plants become unattractively straggly. Prune in early spring to encourage more compact growth. Feed once a month with half strength tomato fertilizer rather than a house plant fertilizer in order to induce sturdy growth and plenty of flowers rather than leaves.

In the flowering period, give water freely. In the winter, give just enough to prevent the compost drying out.

Propagation: With care, shrimp plants may be increased by cuttings. When you prune the plant in spring, trim the cuttings to 5-7.5 cm (2-3 inches) in length. Dip into hormone rooting powder and insert in individual pots of equal parts of peat and sand. Cover the pots with polythene bags to conserve moisture, and keep at about 20°C (68°F). Pot on into John Innes No. 2 potting compost when they have rooted well.

Pests and Diseases: Beloperones may be affected by red spider mites or whitefly.

Bougainvillea and Beloperone guttata (front)

BOUGAINVILLEA**

The bougainvillea or 'paper flower' provides a glorious display of colour. It needs the support of canes or a frame. Like poinsettias, the flowers are insignificant – it is the papery bracts surrounding them that provide colour – pink, red, magenta or orange. The flowering period usually lasts from June to late August.

General Care: Bougainvilleas need as much light as possible during the active growing season. A temperature of about 18-20°C (65-68°F) is ideal and a fairly humid environment is essential. Mist regularly with tepid water during spring and summer and take care to prevent the compost drying out between waterings. Good drainage is essential, however, and the pot must not sit in a saucer of water for long periods. Weekly feeding with a diluted tomato fertilizer will promote flowering.

Over winter, keep the plant on the dry side at a temperature of around 10-13°C (50-55°F). In spring, prune lightly, reducing the plant by a quarter of its height to encourage bushy, well-shaped growth.

Propagation: To succeed with bougainvillea cuttings you will need a propagator that can provide a constant bottom heat of 21-24°C (70-75°F). Take 7.5-10 cm (3-4 inch) cuttings in summer and insert in 5 cm (2 inch) pots of 4 parts seed compost to 1 part sand. Keep in the case until rooted – about three weeks – and allow the young plants to adjust gradually to room conditions.

Pests and Diseases: Aphids, mealy bugs or red spider mites may attack the plant.

BULBS, SPRING*

Spring bulbs provide a superb display of colour at an otherwise drab time of year and require very little care and attention. Apart from the usual hyacinths, you can also grow tulips, crocus, iris, daffodils and narcissi. They will grow in pots, troughs or bowls and are at home in cool situations less hospitable to other plants.

General Care: Plant the bulbs in September or October, singly or in groups, in containers of seed or potting compost. Be careful about mixing varieties – they are unlikely to flower together. Bulbs such as crocus, tulips, daffodils and narcissi, should be planted with their tops about 5 cm (2 inches) below the surface of the compost. Hyacinths should be planted with their tops above the surface. The compost should be kept relatively moist and cool, at around 7°C (45°F), in a dark place. Alternatively, cover container to keep it dark.

When the shoots are 5 cm (2 inches) tall, uncover and place in a well-lit, cool position. A temperature of about 10-13°C (50-55°F) is ideal. Do not allow the compost to dry out. Within a few weeks the bulbs will flower. After flowering, simply put the bulbs outside and let the foliage die down. As bulbs may not flower in pots the next year it is worth buying new ones and planting the old bulbs in the garden.

Propagation: The best method is from offsets. These can be taken from the parent plant and potted. They usually flower about two years later.

Pests and Diseases: Indoor bulbs are usually trouble-free.

LEFT: Two forms each of Calceolaria (left) and Campanula isophylla (right)
RIGHT: Chrysanthemums

CALCEOLARIA*

The unusual flowers of the calceolaria look like half-inflated balloons of bright yellow, orange or red. The flowers are often spotted or streaked and are borne on short stems to produce a low-growing, compact rosette-shaped plant.

Calceolarias last fairly well indoors and usually flower in spring and summer for two or three months. They are best disposed of after flowering.

General Care: Calceolarias will not give of their best in warm, dry conditions. They prefer a fairly cool, light position such as a north-facing windowsill. A temperature of between 10-15°C (50-60°F) is best. Temperatures may well rise during summer, but this will not seriously affect the plant – it is only troubled by constant high temperatures. Always keep the compost relatively moist. Occasional feeding with diluted tomato fertilizer will encourage the plant to remain fairly stocky and to carry a good show of flowers.

Propagation: Calceolaria seed should be germinated from May to July in half pots or seed trays filled with seed compost. Keep it around 18°C (65°F) until germinated and grow on until large enough to handle. At this stage, prick out the seedlings and pot up singly into 9-13 cm (3½-5 inches) pots of potting compost.

Pests and Diseases: Calceolaria are often attacked by aphids and whitefly.

CAMPANULA

The campanula grown as a houseplant is *Campanula isophylla*, commonly called the 'bell flower'. It is an interesting little plant, with blue or white flowers, borne on long stems, which have a tendency to trail. *Campanula isophylla* is usually grown in a pot but, the white form in particular, is most effective as part of a mixed arrangement in a hanging basket.

General Care: *Campanula isophylla* is relatively easy to grow, but it does prefer a fairly cool, light, airy situation and dislikes hot, dry conditions. It will thrive in slightly shaded situations, as well as full light. An ideal position is therefore on a windowsill, screened by a net curtain. During the spring and summer keep the compost relatively moist, but take care to avoid overwatering.

Towards the end of the summer, the plant will cease flowering and should then be trimmed back and kept on the dry side throughout winter, at a minimum temperature of 7°C (45°F). In early spring, the plant will appreciate warmer conditions.

Propagation: Take cuttings, about 5-7.5 cm (2-3 inches) long in April. Dip into rooting hormone and insert in a mixture of 2 parts seed compost to 1 part fine sand. To obtain best results, insert three to five cuttings per 9 cm (3½ inch) pot and grow on in the same pot after rooting.

Pests and Diseases: Aphids may attack campanulas.

CHRYSANTHEMUM*

'A-Y-R Pot Mums' as they are often called – All Year Round Pot Chrysanthemums – are unique in many ways. They give the same effect as a long-lasting bunch of flowers before passing their best and being relegated to the garden or thrown away.

The pot chrysanthemum is available in various colours from popular bright yellow to pink, bronze and red.

General Care: Pot chrysanthemums should never be purchased with flower buds that are too tight; often they suffer a shock in transit and fail to open once you have got them home. Choose a plant with flowers just beginning to open. When you get the plant home, place it in a well-lit situation and water regularly and moderately. Don't allow the plant to dry out or the flowers will fail to open. Given its favourite temperature of about 18°C (65°F), the chrysanthemum should stay in flower for a number of weeks.

After flowering don't throw the chrysanthemum away if you have a space for it in your garden. Try planting it out – the following year it will probably flower again, but at a different time. You will be surprised to see how tall it grows. Though only about 30 cm (12 inches) high as a potted houseplant, in the garden it will probably achieve a height of about 1 metre (3 ft). This increased growth is not due to the garden soil, but to the fact that the houseplant was treated with a chemical to keep it compact. When, after a few months, the effects of this chemical wear off, the plant starts to grow to its normal height.

Propagation: There is not much point in trying to propagate your own a-y-r chrysanthemums. To achieve plants like those you can buy in the shops you would need to adjust day length, using black-out material or artificial light, depending on time of year, and special dwarfing chemicals.

Pests and Diseases: Aphids, red spider mites, thrips and leaf miners may attack; powdery mildew can be a problem if the air temperature is high and the compost too dry.

COLUMNEA**

Few trailing plants give flowers; of those that do, none is as beautiful as the columnea, with its magnificent flame red flowers streaked with yellow, projecting like trumpets from its long stem of tiny paired leaves.

General Care: If you have a warm, reasonably well-lit bathroom or kitchen where the temperature is about 20°C (68°F) and there is sufficient ceiling space to hang a columnea, you will be delighted by the colourful display that it will give each year. A bathroom or kitchen is best because the columnea thrives in a relatively moist environment. Although the plant needs light, prolonged exposure to direct sunlight will discolour and scorch the leaves.

While columneas like a relatively moist atmosphere, too much water in the pot is harmful. Reduce watering to the bare minimum over winter. In this season they can also tolerate a lower temperature – down to about 13°C (55°F). After this cooler period, columnea will gently break into a massive display of flowers that grow out of little green tubes cascading down the lengths of the trails.

If the plant gets unmanageably long, simply trim back the trails to an acceptable length.

Propagation: Take cuttings and divide them into sections of three or four pairs of leaves, leaving approximately 1-2 cm (½-¾ inch) below the bottom pair. Make sure that you get them the right way round. Dip the cuttings in hormone rooting powder and insert about six cuttings into a 9 cm (3½ inch) pot of seed compost. Cover with a polythene bag to conserve moisture.

When rooted, remove the bag and grow the cuttings on in the pot. Pot the plants up, still together, into a larger pot the following year.

Pests and Diseases: Mealy bugs occasionally attack columneas. Aphids may attack the flowers during spring and summer.

CYCLAMEN**

The cyclamen must be one of the most popular flowering houseplants, producing blooms of white, pink, salmon, mauve, red or lilac over a long period, from early autumn to summer.

General Care: Unfortunately, cyclamen are not the easiest plants to care for. Warm, dry, airless conditions spell the rapid demise of cyclamen and induce the all-too-common sight of a plant that has collapsed, its leaves and flowers drooping around the pot.

Cyclamen prefer cool, light airy conditions with a temperature of about 13°C (55°F). They find it difficult to tolerate central heating. A cool bedroom windowsill or any other light position away from excessive heat is ideal.

Watering is best carried out from below to avoid the risk of botrytis (grey mould fungus) setting in on the corm.

After flowering, the plant will gradually die back to its corm. It can be left for a few weeks to rest; during this period it should be kept on the dry side. After about a month, start to give water again. Once active growth commences, feed every two weeks with a tomato fertilizer to encourage flowering.

The silver-leaved cyclamen is probably the best known type. It is, however, the one most likely to suffer from the normal home environment.

The mini-cyclamen is hardier and more tolerant of household conditions. As the name suggests, it is smaller and the leaves are less colourful than the silver-leaved strain, but its flowers are magnificent; some of them even have a slight scent.

Propagation: Cyclamen is relatively easy to propagate from seed. You can either buy seed or collect your own from the plant. When the flowers have been pollinated, their petals fall off, leaving behind a swollen receptacle where the seeds ripen. When the receptacle has matured, it splits open, exposing the seeds.

Sow seed in half pots of seed compost. Cover the seed with about 3 mm (⅛ inch) of compost and keep it at about 18°C (65°F) until germination has occurred – usually about six to eight weeks. When the seedlings are large enough to handle, carefully prick them out into separate pots and grow on.

Pests and Diseases: Cyclamen are prone to botrytis (grey mould fungus).

GARDENIA***

Gardenia is one of the most highly scented flowering plants, with magnificent creamy-white flowers and glossy dark green leaves. The compact, bushy plant makes a lovely houseplant if you can master its rather demanding requirements.

Gardenia and Columnea

General Care: The gardenia likes a semi-shaded position away from direct sunlight and a temperature of about 20°C (68°F). It also requires a very humid condition and a fairly acid compost. Watering with rainwater is beneficial, but if you cannot collect any, use boiled, cooled tap water. Boiling removes some of the calcium salts from hard water, which gardenias dislike.

Throughout spring and summer, water every two weeks with a half strength solution of tomato fertilizer, to help it produce good quality flowers in profusion. An application or two of Sequestrene during the flowering period will prevent chlorosis, a condition typified by yellow patches between the leaf veins. This is caused by an iron deficiency.

Propagation: It is difficult to propagate gardenias from cuttings but worth a try. Take tip cuttings with three or four leaves and dip the base of the stems into hormone rooting powder. Insert the cuttings in individual pots containing 4 parts peat and 1 part sand. Cover each pot with a polythene bag and keep at about 21°C (70°F) until rooted. Reduce the temperature to 18°C (64°F) and keep the pots away from direct sunlight.

Pests and Diseases: Gardenias are sometimes attacked by red spider mites and mealy bugs. Aphids attack the flower buds and young growth.

HIBISCUS**

One of the most exotic and attractive plants is the hibiscus or Chinese rose. The green-leaved species, *Hibiscus rosa-sinensis*, produces flowers in various hues of pink, red or salmon; the variety 'Cooperi' has leaves variegated with cream and crimson, and fewer flowers.

General Care: Do not be discouraged if the flowers of the hibiscus only last a day or so; this is quite normal and a healthy plant produces so many flowers in succession that their short life is not a problem. Some of the flower buds may drop off prematurely, but again this is no cause for concern unless the plant loses more buds than it keeps.

The hibiscus dislikes draughts or great fluctuations in temperature either of which can cause a dramatic bud drop. Aim for a constant room temperature of 18°C (65°F). As the plant loves sunlight, give it as much as possible. But take care if you place it near a window; move it at night as the temperature will drop sharply in that position.

Watering is very important. The plant prefers to be kept moist. Strike a balance between letting it dry out and overwatering. Feed once every two to four weeks from April to September with a half strength tomato fertilizer. In winter, the plant may lose most if not all of its leaves and look very bare and leggy. In spring, prune the plant back by about half to give it a good shape for the new season: it should flower again.

Propagation: Hibiscus can be propagated from cuttings. Take tip cuttings approximately 7.5-10 cm (3-4 inches) from new growth. Dip in hormone rooting powder and insert in 9 cm (3½ inch) pots filled with seed compost. Cover with a polythene bag to conserve moisture and keep at 21°C (70°F). When rooted, remove the bag and pot up in an 11 cm (4½ inch) or a 13cm (5 inch) pot, using a potting compost, and grow on. Trim lightly to encourage a good shape.

Pests and Diseases: Aphids on leaves and flower buds are the major pests; red spider mite may also be a problem.

HYDRANGEA*

Hydrangeas have long been popular as houseplants, even though their life indoors is only a few weeks. A wide range of varieties is now available including lace-caps and the traditional types in blue, pink and white.

General Care: Hydrangeas are outdoor plants forced to flower early for use as houseplants. They therefore prefer a cool light position and are happy in an unheated porch, or a conservatory if the temperature is low enough: 7-15°C (45-60°F) is the acceptable range.

Watering is crucial. Dehydration and collapse will rapidly occur if they are allowed to dry out. Plunge in a bucket of tepid water (rainwater is best) at least once a week. Keep pot submerged until the bubbling stops; remove and drain.

After flowering, hydrangeas can be planted in a sheltered spot in the garden and left to grow with the minimum of attention. Prune once a year and give a twice-yearly application of Sequestrene to prevent chlorosis, a deficiency of iron that causes yellowing between the veins.

Blue hydrangeas often turn pink as the soil condition changes from acid to slightly alkaline. To correct this incorporate sphagnum moss peat to help increase acidity, and water the plant once or twice a year with a solution of alum. This chemical helps to increase acidity and to intensify the blue colour. Alum, or aluminium sulphate, is sold as a blueing compound. Follow manufacturers directions for use. Do not try to 'blue' white or pink varieties.

Feed with a tomato fertilizer once a month during the growing season to promote growth and good flowers.

Propagation: Hydrangeas can be easily propagated from tip or stem cuttings taken from May to July. Remove a stem and cut into pieces, leaving two pairs of leaves on the top cutting and one pair on each stem cutting, with about 3 cm (1½ inches) of stem beneath.

Dip the stem into hormone rooting powder and insert singly into pots of a mixture of equal parts peat and a loam-seed compost. Cover each one with a polythene bag to conserve moisture. Remove the bag when the cuttings have rooted, and pot on.

Pests and Diseases: Hydrangeas are prone to attack from aphids, red spider mites, mildew and eelworm. The latter deforms leaves; infected plants are best destroyed.

White, pink and blue Hydrangeas, and Hibiscus (front)

IMPATIENS*

Impatiens, more popularly known as 'busy Lizzie' is still one of the best loved flowering houseplants. While the familiar plain green-leaved type with pale-pink or rose-pink flowers holds its own, variegated varieties are available.

General Care: Easily maintained, impatiens need little special treatment apart from lots of water. Place the plant in a light situation, but not in direct sunlight behind glass. Do not allow the soil to dry out. During the flowering period, from April to September, feed the plant once every two or three weeks with half strength tomato fertilizer.

To prevent the plant becoming straggly, trim it occasionaly or pinch out the growing points. This helps to keep the plant compact and well-shaped. A more drastic pruning in early spring will ensure that the plant remains a good shape.

Propagation: Busy Lizzies are very easy to propagate. Simply take a 7.5-10 cm (3-4 inch) cutting from a top shoot and root it in a pot of compost after dipping in hormone rooting powder, or in a jar of water. In either case, pot up as soon as rooted.

Pests and Diseases: Aphids and whitefly are the most likely troublemakers; the plants may also be infected by mildew and attacked by red spider mites.

RIGHT: Jasmine
OPPOSITE: Plain and variegated Impatiens

JASMINE*

The jasmine, *Jasminum polyanthum*, is a most rewarding plant to grow, proffering a magnificent display of gorgeous scented flowers from February until April, with very little attention.

General Care: The jasmine prefers a cool well-lit position; it dislikes central heating. Provided the plant is protected from frost, it is remarkably hardy. Do not allow it to dry out, but keep a close watch on its water requirements – it does drink thirstily. Although jasmine can be trained up a cane or along wires, it looks at its best with the flowers entwined around a hoop.

After flowering, from about April to September, feed the plant once a month with half strength tomato fertilizer.

Propagation: Take stem cuttings, dip them in hormone rooting powder and insert in pots of seed compost. Propagate in the spring or autumn for best results; during summer the cuttings will often dehydrate before rooting.

Pests and Diseases: Aphids are the only pest likely to cause trouble, attacking the flower buds and young growth during spring and summer.

POINSETTIA*

The 'flowers' of poinsettias are in fact modified leaves called bracts. The range of colours extend from white or cream, through pink to the colour which everyone knows, bright red.

General Care: Poinsettias should be kept at about 18°C (65°F), well away from draughts. They like plenty of light but should be moved away from a window at night during the winter when they are in colour, for they are very sensitive to low temperatures and temperature fluctuations. As the temperature drops, so do the leaves, followed eventually by the bracts.

Care should also be taken with watering. Although they should not be allowed to dry right out, they must not be overwatered, or the roots will suffocate. This will cause the leaves to yellow and curl, followed eventually by leaf and bract drop.

The flowers of the poinsettia are the little pips in the centre of the bracts. These are shortlived and very soon drop off. After 'flowering', prune the plant in April or May by removing one third to one half of the growth so that the plant will start to 'break'. As the new shoots grow, feed the plant every week with tomato fertilizer at half strength. If the plant starts to outgrow its pot, transfer it to a larger one.

At the end of September, do not allow the plant to be exposed to any artificial light after the hours of daylight, otherwise it will not form its coloured bracts. Poinsettias by nature respond to the shortening autumn days by changing colour. Artificial light during the hours of darkness makes the plant behave as if it is still summer!

Propagation: Poinsettias can be propagated by taking tip cuttings consisting of a shoot with about three or four mature leaves. Dip this into hormone rooting powder and then into a small pot of 4 parts peat to 1 part sand. Cover with a polythene bag and keep at around 21°C (70°F) until rooted. This normally takes three to four weeks. When the roots are established, pot the plant on into a larger container of potting compost.

Pests and Diseases: Whitefly, the major pests of poinsettias, are more unsightly than harmful, but should be dealt with before they get out of hand.

POLYANTHUS*

The diminutive polyanthus heralds spring. Its low-growing rosettes of leaves sport a stem of magnificently coloured flowers of yellow, pink, red, white or blue.

General Care: Polyanthus could not be easier to grow, if you remember that they are derived from outdoor plants and treat them accordingly.

Give them plenty of light and keep them cool. The polyanthus likes water and will soon tell you when it wants more by flagging. Fortunately, if you water the plant promptly, it will quickly recover its former glory.

When it has finished flowering, plant the polyanthus out in the garden. It will quickly adapt to its new environment, and the following spring and summer will provide some of the earliest colour in the garden.

Propagation: Raise from seed sown in a seed tray or half pot of seed compost and lightly covered. Keep at about 18°C (65°F). Once the seedlings are large enough to handle, gently prick them out and pot up singly in 9 cm (3½ inch) pots of potting compost.

Pests and Diseases: Aphids are a year-round problem on flowers and young leaves. In winter botrytis (grey mould) may strike, if damp, dark conditions prevail.

SAINTPAULIA**

Saintpaulias or African violets are very attractive little plants that form a close rosette of fleshy, hairy leaves and produce flowers in a wide range of colours. Although saintpaulias are most commonly known for their deep purple/blue flowers, they are also available in white, pink, wine-red, light blue, dark blue and even bi-coloured and frilled forms.

General Care: Unfortunately, African violets are not very easy to keep. They prefer a temperature of about 20°C (68°F), away from draughts and direct sunlight. Since in their natural habitat they grow on the jungle floor, receiving only mottled light, you will have more chance of success if you place them in the centre of the room, away from the window. Humidity is also important; many people grow them well in kitchens or bathrooms. Humidity can also be increased by plunging the plant still in its pot into another larger pot filled with moist peat.

African violets must be watered from below. Place the plant in a saucer of water and allow it to soak up what it requires within about 20 minutes before pouring away the surplus. Dust can be removed from the hairy leaves by gently dabbing them with a moistened paper kitchen towel. Do not use cold water or allow water to drop on the leaves as this will disfigure them either by cold 'scorch' or the droplets acting as magnifying lenses for the sun's rays.

Stubborn African violets can be coaxed into flower by a very simple technique. Keep the plant on the dry side for six to eight weeks, watering only if it looks like drying out and dying. Gradually increase the water, and feed every two weeks with tomato fertilizer at about quarter strength. This should do the trick!

Propagation: It is fairly simple to propagate African violets from leaf cuttings. Select a semi-mature leaf, and cut it off cleanly at the base of the leaf stalk close to the centre of the plant. Cut back the leaf stalk to about 3-4 cm (1½ inches) and lightly dip into hormone rooting powder. Gently insert the stalk into a 5 cm (2 inch) pot of seed compost, leaving a small space between the base of the leaf and the compost surface. Cover the leaf with a polythene bag and be patient. Rooting may take six to eight weeks and it may be as long again before a plantlet emerges from the base. Pot on the new plant into a 9 cm (3½ inch) pot of potting compost.

Pests and Diseases: African violets sometimes suffer from aphids and mildew during spring and summer; the latter is more difficult to control. All through the year they are prone to botrytis (grey mould). Keep a close watch on the ageing flowers and leaves for the first signs of infection.

SOLANUM*

What makes the solanum or winter cherry ornamental is not its flowers but a display of round, bright orange cherry-like fruits in winter. The small white flowers of summer are insignificant. The plant may reach 45 cm (18 inches) in height and is fairly compact. Deep green foliage sets off the berries well. Although the solanum is from the same family as the tomato and the potato, its fruits are inedible – indeed they are poisonous.

General Care: Solanum can be grown for more than one season, although most people

lispose of them once the fruits ıave dropped. They are very asy to grow provided there is lenty of light and the plants re not allowed to dry right ut, particularly when in flowr or after fruit has set. During pring and summer, a temperture of about 15-18°C (605°F) is ideal; they may even be ept outside from the end of Лay to the end of August. eeding with diluted tomato fertilizer throughout the growing season will help to encourage stocky growth and a good covering of flowers – hopefully followed by berries. Fruit set can be increased indoors by lightly misting the plant with tepid water or by tickling the flowers with an artist's paintbrush to pollinate them. Over winter, solanum will tolerate a temperature down to around 10°C (50°F).

Various shades of Saintpaulia

Propagation: Sow seed in early spring in a half pot or seed tray of seed compost, cover and keep at 18-20°C (65-68°F). When the seedlings are large enough to handle, prick out and pot up singly in 13 cm (5 inch) pots of potting compost.
Pests and Diseases: Aphids and whitefly may attack.

STEPHANOTIS**

The stephanotis is a climbing plant that is usually grown on a hoop so that the scented waxy white flowers of this thick, fleshy green-leaved plant may be displayed to their best advantage.

General Care: A temperature of 20°C (68°F) is ideal. A reasonably well-lit situation, away from direct sunlight, will provide the right growing conditions. Take care to avoid draughts as this can cause premature leaf or flower drop.

Over the dormant winter period, keep the plant on the dry side. During the active growing and flowering period, do not allow it to dry out. A monthly feed with half strength tomato fertilizer promotes stocky growth and good flower cover.

Propagation: Propagate from stem cuttings taken from non flowering side shoots in early summer. Dip 10 cm (4 inch) cuttings in hormone rooting powder and insert in a half pot of seed compost. If you keep at about 18°C (65°F), they should root in a few weeks. Pot on as necessary.

Pests and Diseases: Mealy bugs are the main pest and can be rather difficult to control when the plant grows more densely on its hoop.

Stephanotis, with its tubular flowers, behind two forms of Streptocarpus

STREPTOCARPUS*

Popularly known as the Cape primrose, this plant bears pink, red, purple or lilac flowers. The mid-green leaves are very like primrose leaves but larger and tend to grow haphazardly rather than in a neat rosette, giving a bushy background to the lovely summer blooms.

General Care: While flowering in spring and summer, streptocarpus prefer a temperature of around 15-18°C (60-65°F) in a lightly shaded situation away from direct sunlight. Do not allow the plants to dry out between May and October but keep them fairly dry for the winter, maintaining a temperature of 10-13°C (50-55°F). From March onwards, as temperatures gradually rise again, water more frequently.

Propagation: Streptocarpus are easily propagated from seed or leaf cuttings. During spring and summer, sow seed in half pots or seed trays filled with seed compost and keep covered at about 21°C (70°F) until germinated. When the seedlings are large enough to handle, prick them out and pot up singly in 13 cm (5 inch) pots of John Innes No. 2 potting compost.

Streptocarpus cuttings are worth trying for fun. Select a semi-mature leaf and cut it off cleanly. Using a sharp knife and a chopping board, lay the leaf flat on the board and cut in half down the central main vein. Cut each half into pieces about 2.5 cm (1 inch) wide, cutting upwards from the main vein to the leaf edge. Dip the cut edge of the main vein into rooting hormone and lightly insert in half pots or seed trays filled with seed compost. Mist with tepid water several times a day, or cover with a polythene bag, to reduce water loss. When the cuttings have rooted pot up singly in 9 cm (3½ inch) pots of growing compost and grow on.

Pests and Diseases: Aphids very occasionally attack streptocarpus.

THUNBERGIA*

Thunbergia or 'black-eyed Susan' is an annual climbing and trailing plant that provides a useful if short-lived display of golden-orange flowers with a brownish-black centre or 'eye'. A rapid grower, it will need to be kept in check if it is not to become untidy. It can easily grow to a height of 1 metre (3 ft) in a good position. The mid-green foliage of thunbergia provides a modest foil for the profusion of flowers.

General Care: Thunbergia is very easy to grow in a cool, light position – indeed it can be grown outside from the end of May when all danger of frosts has passed. Keep the plant well watered and never let it dry out at any time. Feeding with diluted tomato fertilizer will encourage flowering. The support of a cane, trellis or wire frame is essential. As soon as flowering is over, dispose of the plant.

Propagation: Since propagation from seed is very easy you can quickly grow your own thunbergia to flower within a few months. In March, sow about four seeds in a 13 cm (5 inch) pot of seed compost and germinate at about 20°C (68°F). Pot up individually in 11 cm (4 inch) pots of John Innes No. 2 potting compost and grow on.

Pests and Diseases: Aphids and whitefly may attack.

Thunbergia

CACTI, SUCCULENTS & BROMELIADS

Cacti, succulents and bromeliads are an extraordinary collection of plants. They share one important characteristic – an excellent adaptability to their environment.

Cacti and other succulents have thick fleshy leaves designed to conserve moisture. They are able to tolerate both extremes of temperature and long periods without water. Although their natural habitat is the desert, these plants will not grow in pure sand; they require sand containing soil.

Bromeliads, or 'tree pineapples' as they are often called, live on trees in the rain forests of the world. There they exist as epiphytes (tree living plants), anchored to – and collecting all of their material needs from – the branch of a tree. Rainwater and detritus are collected in a central funnel which is formed by broad, strap-like leaves radiating from the centre of the plant. This funnel is the main source of water for bromeliads.

Because cacti, succulents and bromeliads are adaptable, they are relatively easy to look after. Bromeliads have attractive leaves – plain or variegated – and many produce magnificent flowerheads which last for many weeks. Although cacti are usually kept for their unusual forms, many of them flower regularly, providing brilliant displays of colour at different times of the year.

Unless they are very fine specimens, cacti do not create a striking display in individual pots. They are much more effective in group cacti arrangements. Cacti are not suitable for mixing with other types of plants because their water requirements are different.

AECHMEA FASCIATA*

The aechmea or urn plant is a member of the bromeliad or tree pineapple family. Its large, greenish grey strap-like leaves radiate upwards and outwards. At their centre, where water collects, the large pink flower spike emerges. The spike produces flowers of violet-blue turning to rose-pink that are relatively short-lived. They are, however, produced in succession and the flower spike can live for as long as six months. They normally appear in autumn.

General Care: Aechmeas are relatively easy to look after. A semi-shaded position away from direct sunlight is best, with a temperature of about 15-18°C (60-65°F); they will tolerate lower temperatures, however. During the growing period, give the plants rainwater (if possible) in the central funnel and in the compost. Although the compost may be allowed to dry out, do not let the funnel run dry. Remove the flower spike when it has faded by gently pulling; if it does not come away easily, do not tug too hard, but wait a little longer. Clean the leaves by rinsing them with tepid water. Never wipe them with a cloth, for this removes the decorative banding.

Propagation: Once the plant has finished flowering, it will usually produce one or more offsets. When these have grown to approximately one third to one half the size of the parent, moisten the compost well and gently tease the offsets away, potting them up singly in 13 cm (5 inch) pots, using a lime-free compost.

Pests and Diseases: Aechmeas are sometimes attacked by root mealy bugs and aphids on the flower spike, but generally they are trouble-free.

AGAVE*

The agaves are succulent plants which grow wild in Mexico and the warmer parts of North America. All members of the agave family carry their well-defined succulent sword-shaped leaves in the form of a rosette. One of the most attractive varieties is *Agave americana* 'Marginata', with its variegated green and cream leaves. *Agave victoriae-reginae*, which has dark green fleshy leaves with white margins, also makes a striking sight.

General Care: Some tougher agaves can be grown outside for most of the year but they need to be protected from frost. They must, however, be given full light and kept on the dry side. Excessively wet conditions spell the rapid demise of the plant. Agaves may eventually flower from the centre of the rosette. After

Aechmea fasciata and Agave

flowering most agaves will produce offsets around their bases and then die. *Agave victoriae-reginae* does not produce offsets.

Propagation: Carefully remove young plants produced around the base of the plant and pot them singly in 13 cm (5 inch) pots of John Innes No. 2 potting compost. Spring is the best time to do this. Agaves can also be propagated from seed in the same way as Aloes (see opposite).

Pests and Diseases: Mealy bugs and sometimes root mealy bugs attack agaves, but they are troubled by very little else.

ALOE*

The aloe produces a rosette of leaves in a spiral formation from which the slender flower stem emerges. The flowers are bell-shaped, coloured yellow, orange and red.

Aloe variegata is the most common variety; it has attractively variegated leaves of very dark green and white.

General Care: Aloes prefer a well-lit situation and a temperature of around 18°C (65°F). They will adapt, however, to a wide range of temperatures. Keep the plant rather dry, particularly in winter. It will rot if kept too moist.

Propagation: Aloes can be propagated from offsets. These can easily be separated from the plant and potted up singly. They can also be raised from seed. Germinate the seed in a mixture of 4 parts seed compost to 1 part fine sand at about 18°C (68°F); prick out the young plants when they are large enough to handle and pot up singly in a similar mixture.

Pests and Diseases: Aloes are sometimes troubled by mealy bugs and root mealy bugs.

Echeveria and Cryptanthus (front)

CRYPTANTHUS**

The cryptanthus or earth star is a diminutive low-growing bromeliad that is ideal for use in bottle gardens or plant arrangements. It is available in a wide range of colours and produces small flowers, usually white, from the centre of its rosette of leaves. The shade and intensity of the leaves can be affected by light.

General Care: The native habitat of cryptanthus is the floor of a tropical rain forest. They therefore prefer a humid environment in semi-shade with a temperature of about 16-18°C (61-65°F). Keep them evenly moist without overwatering, but do not worry if they dry right out, for these plants are very resilient.

Cryptanthus can be planted in bottle gardens or in individual pots. They have a disconcerting feature; the young plantlets produced from their centre seem to jump off at the slightest knock. This is the plant's natural method of reproducing itself. Give it a position where it is out of harm's way and deal with it gently.

Propagation: Detach a plantlet from the mother plant, or use one that has fallen off. Fill a 9 cm (3½ inch) pot with seed compost and gently press the base of the plantlet into the compost. Then just leave it to root, making sure that the compost does not dry out. Be patient; rooting can take up to six months.

Pests and Diseases: Mealy bugs and root mealy bugs very occasionally attack the cryptanthus.

CONOPHYTUM**

Conophytums or cone plants are extraordinary succulents that look like the small pebbles among which they grow in their native habitat. For this reason they, and the similar species *Lithops*, are known as living stones. There are several conophytum species available, with different coloured flowers – yellow, orange, red and pink. The flowers emerge from the centre of the fleshy body.

General Care: To encourage these plants to flower, keep them cool and dry in winter, watering a little from March/April onwards and stopping in May/June. In July/August, resume watering; in September/October flowers should appear. After flowering, the plant will re-enter its winter dormancy and the cycle begins again. New growth will appear beneath the old skin, which gradually shrivels and turns brown. Remove it gently with tweezers when it is ready to come away. When actively growing, conophytums need plenty of light, air, and a temperature around 20°C (68°F).

Propagation: Conophytums increase naturally forming larger and larger clumps. They can therefore be propagated by division. Simply detach individual plantlets and insert individually in pots containing a mixture of 4 parts seed compost to 1 part fine sand.

Pests and Diseases: Although mealy bugs and root mealy bugs may attack, they are fairly easy to deal with because the plants are so small.

ECHEVERIA*

The echeveria is a succulent that forms a compact rosette of leaves and bears flowers of white, yellow-orange or red. *Echeveria setosa*, with hairy leaves, is one of the most common varieties, and can be grown outside in the summer.

General Care: Echeverias are tough little plants but they have certain preferences. In summer they need plenty of water; in winter they should be kept just moist. Do not get water on the leaves or they will be marked. The plants like to spend summer outdoors in the sun and air. Bring them indoors in winter and let them have plenty of light, but a low temperature of 5°C (41°F).

Propagation: Echeverias can be propagated quite easily from cuttings by gently pulling or cutting off a leaf and inserting it in a mixture of 4 parts seed compost to 1 part sand. Use the same mixture to raise echeverias from seed.

Pests and Diseases: Mealy bugs and root mealy bugs may attack, but echevarias are usually trouble-free.

ECHINOCACTUS GRUSONII*

The echinocactus is sometimes called the golden barrel cactus. It looks just like a barrel, covered in golden spines that can grow up to 7-8 cm (3 inches) long. Flowers are usually small and not often produced in this country.

General Care: Echinocactus, like most cacti, require a position in full light to encourage growth. During spring and summer, water the plant freely; in winter keep it almost dry. A summer temperature of 18°C (65°F) is ideal; during winter 10°C (50°F) is acceptable.

Propagation: Echinocactus are best propagated in spring from seed germinated in a mixture of 4 parts seed compost to 1 part fine sand. Sprinkle sand lightly over the seed. Keep at 20°C (68°F) until germinated. When the seedlings are large enough to handle, prick them out and pot up.

Pests and Diseases: Mealy bugs and root mealy bugs may be troublesome.

Two flowering Mammillaria (page 73) and Echinocactus grusonii (front)

EPIPHYLLUM**

One of the most attractive of the flowering cacti is the epiphyllum or orchid cactus. The beautiful flowers are borne on green, fleshy and often flat-sided stems and vary in size from 5-15 cm (2-6 inches) across. They may be single or double, and coloured white, yellow, pink, orange, red, or lilac. Some of the flowers are fragrant.

General Care: In winter, keep the orchid cactus relatively cool, down to 7°C (45°F), but never let them dry out. In spring and summer, maintain regular watering. Give a liquid feed every two weeks once the flower buds are visible in spring. The best position is one where they can enjoy plenty of light but not the direct sun during mid summer.

Propagation: Epiphyllums can easily be propagated from stem cuttings taken in summer and inserted into pots of seed compost after being dipped in hormone rooting powder. Alternatively, raise them from seed sown in spring in a mixture of 4 parts seed compost to 1 part sand and germinate at 20°C (68°F). Prick out the seedlings when they are large enough to handle and later pot on.

Pests and Diseases: Epiphyllums are subject to attack by mealy bugs and root mealy bugs; aphids occasionally infest the flowers.

Hoya bella and Euphorbia (front)

EUPHORBIA MILII**

Known as the crown of thorns this relative of the poinsettia has woody stems clothed with sharp thorns. Its colourful 'flowers' are in fact bracts, and are generally rose-pink but sometimes pale yellow.

General Care: Keep at about 18°C (65°F) during the spring and summer in full sun and with good ventilation. Water freely but not to excess. In winter, give just enough water to keep the compost moist. Do not let the temperature drop below 13°C (55°F). Place in good light away from draughts.

Propagation: The preferable method is from seed, sown in a 4 to 1 ratio of seed compost to fine sand. Keep at 20°C (68°F). *Euphorbia milii* can also be propagated by cuttings dipped into rooting hormone and then planted into a similar compost at a similar temperature. However, try to avoid this method, because cutting the plant releases the milky latex-like sap which is an irritant to the eyes and skin.

Pests and Diseases: The sap discourages most pests but mealy bugs sometimes attack.

HOYA BELLA*

Hoya bella is a super little trailing plant with small spear-shaped fleshy green leaves. Its delightful flowers are produced in summer in clusters of porcelain white with pink centres. They are seen to best advantage if the pot is in a hanging basket.

General Care: *Hoya bella* prefers a situation out of direct sunlight. Take care to avoid overwatering, otherwise root rotting may occur. In winter, keep it on the dry side at a temperature of 13-15°C (55-60°F). In spring and summer, a temperature of 18-20°C (65-68°F) and a humid atmosphere is preferred. Give water more frequently and spray with a fine mist of tepid water on hot days. Pinch out the growing tips to prevent the plant from becoming leggy.

Propagation: Take 7.5 cm (3 inch) stem cuttings in June. Dip the bottom of the stems into hormone rooting powder and insert five to each 9 cm (3½ inch) pot of seed compost. Keep at 16-18°C (61-65°F) until rooted. Allow to grow on in the same pot.

Pests and Diseases: *Hoya bella* may be troubled by mealy bugs and root mealy bugs.

Neoregelia carolinae 'Tricolor' *(page 74)*

MAMMILLARIA*

Mammillaria is the most commonly grown species of cactus. They are covered with nipple-like tubercules that give the plant its name. These are arranged in whorls that spiral around the plant. *Mammillaria hahniana* and *Mammillaria zeilmanniana* are two of the most popular. Both bear red flowers in a ring at the top of the plant. Other varieties have white, yellow or pink flowers.

General Care: Mammillarias need to be in full sun in order to flower. In summer, water generously without soaking; in winter, let the compost dry out and do not let the temperature drop below 7°C (45°F).

Propagation: In May and August offsets are produced which can be gently teased away from the parent. Let them dry for a day and pot up in a mixture of 4 parts seed compost to 1 part fine sand.

Alternatively, in spring they can be raised from seed sown in a similar compost, lightly covered with fine sand and kept at 20°C (68°F) until germinated. When seedlings are large enough to handle, prick them out and pot up.

Pests and Diseases: Mealy bugs and root mealy bugs may be a problem.

NEOREGELIA*

The neoregelia is a magnificent bromeliad with glossy green and white striped strap-like leaves that are held prostrate by the plant and join to form a cup at their base. In the form generally seen as a houseplant, *Neoregelia carolinae* 'Tricolor', the leaves are bright rose-pink at their base. At flowering time, which tends to be spring, this colour radiates outwards from the centre, and the whole plant may change colour. Lilac-pink flowers appear just above the pool of water in the middle.

General Care: Neoregelias are easy to keep because they are so adaptable. A lightly shaded situation away from direct sunlight is best with a temperature around 15-18°C (60-65°F) although temperatures down to 10°C (50°F) can be tolerated. The funnel should always be kept topped up with water, rainwater if you can provide it. In summer, water frequently without soaking; in winter keep the compost just moist. After flowering, the plant will devote all of its enegry to producing offshoots and the old parent plant will die soon afterwards.

Propagation: Let the offshoots make roots while still attached to the parent plant. Sever them in June or July and put them in individual 13 cm (5 inch) pots of equal parts sand and medium loam. Provide each plantlet with a supporting stake and do not plant too deep; there is a danger of root rot at this early stage of growth. Water sparingly but keep the atmosphere relatively humid until a sound root formation has been made.

Pests and Diseases: Neoregelias are, luckily, usually free from the attentions of pests; root mealy bugs may attack occasionally.

NOTOCACTUS*

The most commonly grown notocactus is *Notocactus leninghausii*, sometimes known as goldfinger cactus. It grows slowly to a magnificent rotund column and produces yellow trumpet-shaped flowers at its top that may reach about 5 cm (2 inches) in diameter. Although spines are not very pronounced, together with the ribs they are visually most impressive.

General Care: Like most cacti, notocactus like full light. In winter keep them cool at a temperature of about 13°C (55°F) and let the compost dry. Summer temperatures of about 18°C (65°F) are best, and allow the compost to dry out between waterings.

Propagation: Notocactus are best propagated from seed in a mixture of 4 parts seed compost to 1 part fine sand. For germination provide a temperature of 20°C (68°F).

It is possible to propagate from a top cutting taken if the plant grows too tall. Let the cutting dry out before putting it in sand to root. When rooted, pot on into a light, porous growing medium.

Pests and Diseases: Mealy bugs and root mealy bugs are the most common pests.

OPUNTIA*

Opuntias are better known as prickly pears or bunny ears. Their stems are like round or oval pads and are covered with fine bristles which will require careful handling. There are many different species, but the most common ones have stems comprising lengths of joined pads protruding at different angles. The flowers vary in colour from yellow to orange and red. One of the most suitable varieties for the home is *Opuntia microdasys*. It is a small plant which produces numerous pads dotted with tiny spines.

General Care: Opuntias are quite easy to grow. They need a rich growing medium and, unlike many cacti, need some water the whole year round – plenty in summer, enough to prevent the compost drying out in winter. If they become dry, brown spots appear on the pads. A minimum winter temperature of 7°C (45°F) is necessary. Repot opuntias annually in spring.

Notocactus

Propagation: The easiest way to propagate opuntias is from the pads taken in June or July. Wear leather gloves and wrap a piece of coarse cloth or paper round the plant to protect your hands from the spines. Simply pull off a pad, let it dry out for two or three days and insert in a pot of John Innes No.2 potting compost. Keep the compost moist but not waterlogged, otherwise the roots may suffocate.
Pests and Diseases: Opuntias may be attacked by mealy bugs and root mealy bugs.

PACHYPODIUM**

Pachypodium is a strange plant that looks like an animated club. It has a swollen spine-covered woody stem, with a cluster of glossy thick leaves at the top. Flowers may be white, yellow, pink or mauve.
General Care: Pachypodiums are more sensitive than other succulents to overwatering; be sparing in this respect and keep an eye on humidity levels. The winter temperature should not be allowed to drop below 13°C (55°F). Aim for a temperature of 18°C (65°F) in summer.
Propagation: Pachypodiums can be raised from seed. In early spring, sow seed in a mixture of 4 parts seed compost to 1 part sand. Cover lightly with fine sand and keep at 20°C (68°F) until germinated. When the seedlings are large enough to handle, prick them out and pot up.
Pests and Diseases: Mealy bugs sometimes attack pachypodiums but few other pests are game enough to take on its tough and woody stem.

PARODIA*

Parodias produce beautiful yellow or red flowers at the top of their globular stems, which grow to about 7.5 cm (3 inches) in diameter.
General Care: Unfortunately, parodias are more difficult to grow than many other cacti and soon react adversely to overwatering. The sensitive roots die quickly if the plant is mistreated. To be safe, keep the plant on the dry side throughout the winter at a minimum temperature of 13°C (55°F). During the spring and summer water sparingly to avoid any problems. If the roots do fail, stop watering immediately and coax the plant to produce new roots by keeping the temperature constant at 18°C (65°F).
Propagation: Seed is the best method of propagation. Raise in the same way as other cacti.
Pests and Diseases: Mealy bugs are the only pest likely to attack parodias.

REBUTIA*

Rebutias are tiny cacti that produce an amazing number of flowers for their size. The low, flattened, globular stems reach no more than 5 cm (2 inches) in diameter but in summer produce a mass of trumpet-like flowers from white to yellow-orange and brilliant red, all around the base of the stem.
General Care: Rebutias are some of the easiest cacti to cultivate and are the ideal plants with which to start a collection. They are happy growing on windowsills in full light and are tolerant of varying conditions. A cool dry winter followed by a warmer and more moist spring and summer are the ideal conditions. The flowers close during the evening but reopen with the next day's light.
Propagation: Rebutias are easy to raise from seed, germinated in the usual way for cacti.
Pests and Diseases: Mealy bugs and root mealy bugs are the main problems; aphids sometimes attack the flowers.

Parodia, Opuntia and Rebutia (front)

SANSEVIERIA*

The variety of sansevieria commonly known as mother-in-law's tongue is *Sansevieria trifasciata* 'Laurentii'. Its familiar upright green and yellow striped leaves grow up to a metre (3 ft) tall.

General Care: The mother-in-law's tongue prefers a well-lit situation at a temperature of about 18°C (65°F); in winter the temperature should not drop below 10°C (50°F) and the compost should then be kept on the dry side. Water infrequently in summer and let the compost dry right out in winter between waterings.

Propagation: Sansevierias are easily propagated by cuttings. Cut a leaf into 5 cm (2 inch) sections and put four or five sections into a pot of moist potting compost. Make sure the cuttings are the right way up. Cover the pot with a polythene bag until plantlets have formed. Remove the bag and pot each plantlet into a 7.5 cm (3 inch) pot of John Innes No.1 potting compost.

Propagation by division is relatively easy but requires a certain degree of courage. Take the plant from its pot and gently tease apart the various pieces. Pot them up singly or in groups in potting compost. Do not, however, be tempted to separate the new shoots that are very small. Leave them until they are at least 10 cm (4 inches) tall before separating them. Water very sparingly after separation for sansevierias are particularly susceptible to overwatering after this procedure.

Pests and Diseases: Sansevierias are normally free from pests and diseases.

SCHLUMBERGERA*

Schlumbergeras or Christmas cacti are normally tree-living cacti. In winter they produce magnificent pink or red blossoms on their flattened stems.

General Care: During the winter, keep the plant at about 13°C (55°F) and do not let the compost dry out; during spring and summer raise the temperature to around 18°C (65°F) and continue to water in moderation. The plant may be stood outside in summer, but avoid direct sunlight; schlumbergeras prefer a little light shade. Avoid draughts, too, or the flower buds or leaf pads may be shed prematurely.

Propagation: Schlumbergeras can easily be propagated from cuttings taken in summer. Cut off a pad near the joint and let it dry out for a few days before inserting in a pot containing equal parts of peat and sand. Cover with a polythene bag until rooted. Gradually accustom the new plant to open-air conditions by perforating the bag to admit a little air before eventually discarding it.

Pests and Diseases: Mealy bugs and root mealy bugs may cause problems.

SELENICEREUS*

The rarely seen but magnificent selenicereus is sometimes called the moon cactus because the flowers open at night. The most popular variety is queen of the night, *Selenicereus grandiflorus,* the flowers of which measure up to 20 cm (8 inches) across and are usually creamy-white tinted scarlet, yellow or mauve and with a heady scent. Because they normally reach 1.8 metres (6 ft) in height they need the support of canes.

General Care: A cool dryish winter temperature, around 13°C (55°F), followed by a spring and summer temperature of about 18°C (65°F) with more frequent waterings will provide reasonable growing conditions. Misting with tepid water will encourage growth.

Propagation: Selenicereus can be propagated from cuttings or seed as for other cacti.

Pests and Diseases: Mealy bugs and root mealy bugs are the most common pests.

STAPELIA**

The stapelia is a succulent whose extraordinary flower has led it to be called the starfish flower because of its shape, or carrion flower because of the unpleasant smell produced by some species. However, species grown as houseplants rarely produce any offensive odour.

General Care: Stapelia are not easy to cultivate. They prefer a minimum winter temperature of 5°C (41°F) and spring and summer temperature of 18-21°C (65-70°F). Great care should be taken to keep the compost on the dry side in winter and not too wet during the spring and summer. Mist occasionally with tepid water in hot, dry weather.

Propagation: Stapelias are easily raised from cuttings. Take cuttings at any time of year, simply by breaking sections off at the base. Let them dry for a day or two, then insert in pots of sand. If you keep the temperature steady at 16°C they should root readily.

Pests and Diseases: Mealy bugs and root mealy bugs are the most common pests.

VRIESIA SPLENDENS*

Vriesia splendens is a bromeliad similar in shape to the aechmea, but its leaves are more slender. Banded dark green and straplike in shape, they form a funnel in the centre of the rosette that collects water. When mature, the plant produces a long orange-red flat-sided flower spike; from this the brightly coloured, but short-lived, flowers emerge.

General Care: Vriesias adapt to a variety of indoor conditions. Although they will tolerate temperatures down to 10°C (50°F), around 18°C (65°F) is best, in a semi-shaded position away from direct sunlight. The plant should be watered in the funnel. Use rainwater if possible, although tap water is perfectly adequate. Try to keep the compost reasonably moist most of the time. When the flower spike dies, gently remove it from the funnel.

Vriesia splendens is an epiphytic or tree-living bromeliad, using its host for support. Adventurous indoor gardeners will find that it adapts well to being grown attached to a branch bound with sphagnum moss in a plant arrangement like a miniature jungle.

Propagation: Vriesia is usually propagated from offsets in the same way as Aechmea (see page 68). Pot the offsets singly in 13 cm (5 inch) pots of lime-free compost.

Pests and Diseases: Root mealy bugs and aphids on the flower spike are the most likely pests.

Vriesia splendens, Sansevieria

INDEX

ACKNOWLEDGMENTS

Photography by Roger Phillips
Photographic stylists: Beverley Behrens
and Penny Markham
Illustrations by Christine Davison,
except those on pages 18 to 22 drawn by Patti Pearce,
both artists from The Garden Studio.

The publishers would also like to thank
Clifton Nurseries and Thomas Rocheford and Sons
for the loan of accessories for photography.

PDO 82-0758